D1102520

THE ROSE AND THE BLADE

THE ROSE AND THE BLADE

New & Selected Poems 1957-1997

JOHN CAMPBELL

LAGAN PRESS
BELFAST
1997

Published by
Lagan Press
PO Box 110 BT12 4AB, Belfast

ARTS
COUNCIL
of Northern Ireland

© John Campbell, 1997

The moral right of the author has been asserted.

A catalogue record of this book is available from the British Library.

ISBN: 1 873687 71 0
Author: Campbell, John
Title: The Rose and the Blade: New and Selected Poems 1957-1997
Format: Paperback (138 mm x 210 mm)
1997

Set in New Baskerville
Printed by Noel Murphy Printing, Belfast

to my family and friends
past and present
home and abroad
alive or dead
but especially to the memory
of my mother and father

CONTENTS

Of York Street & Other Things

When I started writing forty years ago, it was a different world and Belfast a very different place. The York Street area of my childhood was one of the vibrant areas of the city. Its docks were thriving as were its tobacco factory and spinning mills. People poured from its railway station and celebrities like the comedians Stan Laurel and Oliver Hardy stayed in its first-class hotel in Whitla Street. It had timber mills, engineering yards, churches, schoolhouses, cinemas and dancehalls, even a fire and police station—both kept rather busy at times.

In other words, it was a city within a city, a world of its own, and the life of these few streets fascinated me. I loved its teeming life. I loved its characters and its lore. Men streamed from all parts of Belfast and beyond to work on the docks. It had more public houses and betting shops per head than any other part of the city and foreign seamen from all over the world mixed with the locals, enjoying the vibrant atmosphere until it was time to return to their ships, some of which were moored a stone's throw away at the bottom of Dock Street. Now and again the peace of our small world would be shattered as pitched battles broke out between the locals and the foreigners. Only the arrival of the Head Constable and his squad of storm-troopers would halt the brutal skirmishes.

Among the places I remember was the local dancehall called 'The Jig' at the York Street end of North Thomas Street. Often the scene of such donnybrooks and during the war years, fighting men, wearing the uniforms of every country engaged in the conflict could be seen whirling the local girls around the floor. The swing music—played by a live band—was loud enough to be heard streets away. Across the road, in Geordie's cafe, the peelers sat with machine-guns slung around their necks, sipping tea and/or ready to spring at any hint of trouble.

It was exciting to live in York Street in those days. We cadged chewing gum and money from the friendly Yanks, hopped horse-drawn carts that took us to the docks or Alec's Bank, played in the bombed-out houses, or bought a half-penny tram ride to the Duncairn to see the latest potboiler.

Free entertainment could be had by standing at the corner and listening to the local men pontificate on almost every subject under the sun. That's where many of us got streetwise. It was in many ways our classroom, a stern one where our presence was suffered but where we could not take part in the free flowing talk. Children being seen but not heard was no mere adage in those days. Meanwhile, the real head of the family would be toiling away at the kitchen sink, turning the mangle, or making the dinner whilst keeping a wary eye on her young ones. Certainly there was poverty and hard times, but there was also love and affection, family unity and a detached dignity amidst the squalor. There was also a certain innocence that seems to have disappeared forever: just like the York Street I grew up in.

***

And I suppose that's where I—and other writers like me—come in. The growing awareness of the Belfast working-class of their roots and beginnings, reflected in the emergence of locally-produced books and pamphlets, is perhaps not a new phenomenon. It does, however, give a great deal of pleasure to those of us who cherish the traditions and customs of those days gone by. Whether we write in prose, free verse, rhyme or song, our observations must capture on paper the sum and substance of our own lives and the lives of those who came before us. Such writings—containing details of a distinct and local history under threat of being forgotten or erased—are, I feel, an important factor in the fight to preserve our traditions as well as providing a record of our tribulations.

While this is important, however, I hope we are not just creating material for sociologists of the future. In our poems and stories we record the passing or departure of people, places and things that mean a great deal to all of us. It could be the death of a relative or a way of life, the demise of a friend or an era or it could be a record of those events, thoughts and emotions that could happen to any of us—a wedding, hearing a shaggy-dog story, becoming a grandfather, admiring the skill and courage of a boxer, hearing a half-forgotten song, a flight of fancy, a drink on a Saturday night. They are, I suppose, the things that unite us all.

John Campbell
Spring 1997

Publisher's Note

In a writing career spanning forty years, John Campbell has produced three collections of poetry: *Saturday Night in York Street* (1982), *An Oul Jobbin' Poet* (1989) and *Memories of York Street* (1991). The last of these collections recalled and collected specific poems about the York Street area of Belfast. Therefore, it was decided that the section *New Poems 1989-1997* should be those poems written since the publication of *An Oul Jobbin' Poet* in 1989. It has also been decided this section should begin this particular selection. The other books are presented in chronlogical order of appearance. During his writing career, John Campbell has written many poems which were excluded from previous collections for various reasons. A selection of these has been gathered in the final section of the book, *Uncollected Poems 1957-1989.* The poems there have been arranged in chronological order of composition.

from
NEW POEMS
(1989-1997)

THE ROSE AND THE BLADE
for Mandy and Alan on their wedding day

When this marvellous gathering finally ends
and you bid fond farewell to your families and friends
take time to reflect on the vows you have made
as you start life together, a rose and a blade.
In sacred surroundings, between altar and pew,
we smiled as God's words wed your loved one to you.
Without this foundation of mutual trust,
a sweet rose will wilt and a proud blade will rust.
Be steadfast and faithful in all that you do
and the sweet rose will bloom and the blade remain true.

So drink in the grandeur before this day goes
and your guests wander home to contented repose.
Remember the date, every year it comes round,
keep fresh in your memories the fragrance and sound,
the colourful finery worn by each guest,
all sporting carnations or fern on their breast,
the sweet scented posies the young bridesmaids bring,
the warmth in the voices as wedding guests sing
the hymns you requested for this blessed day,
the hearts bound together, as heads bow to pray.

Now celebrations and feasting is due
as your friends and relations pay homage to you.
The Best Man will act with his usual flair,
organizing the toasts to the just married pair.
Each father will feel his offspring has been blessed.
The mothers will weep for chicks leaving the nest.
Some crystallized tear-drops will solemnly fall
and the whirring camcorder will capture it all,
preserving each scene of the marriage just made
of Mandy and Alan ... The Rose and the Blade.

BELFAST PUBLIC LIBRARIES

NORTHERN IRELAND

Northern Ireland is the Lagan flowing to the sea,
It's the leaping trout, a glass of stout,
   It's the forests growing wild and free.
Northern Ireland is the Sperrins, peeping through a mist,
   It's a Portrush Strand with golden sand,
   It's the country lanes that wind and twist.
   It's Derry, with its city walls,
It's the Oul Lammas Fair with its stalls,
   It's Dundrum Bay, the waters of Lough Neagh
That call me when I stray from your shores, Northern Ireland,
   Northern Ireland, my home.

Northern Ireland is a cottage in the heart of Down,
It's a Belfast smile on the Golden Mile,
   It's a horse fair in a market town.
Northern Ireland is the bridge across the River Foyle,
   It's a village pub serving farmyard grub,
   It's Saint Patrick, buried in its soil.
   It's the mountains of Mourne and the Lakes,
The aroma of barbecued steaks.
   It's Old Bushmills, and smoke from poteen stills
That filters through your valleys and hills, Northern Ireland,
   Northern Ireland, my home.

Northern Ireland is Fermanagh's water wonderland,
It's a surf-board ride, an Atlantic tide,
   It's the legend of the severed hand.
Northern Ireland is the breathtaking beauty of Tyrone,
   It's the Glenshane Pass, it's Dungannon glass,
   It's White Island figures carved from stone.
   It's the Glens and the Marble Arch caves,
It's the seabirds afloat on the waves.
   It's a Lambeg drum, the Planetarium,
That make the people come to your shores, Northern Ireland,
   Northern Ireland, my home.

Northern Ireland is its Castles, picturesque and grand.
It's the Strangford Lough, a scenic walk,
   It's a farmer ploughing on his land.
Northern Ireland is Downpatrick, homeland of a Saint,
   It's the Causeway Coast, it's a Customs Post,

It's the townlands, colourful and quaint.
It's Navan, with its ancient fort,
It's the Newcastle seaside resort,
It's Cushendall, a pilgrimage to Saul ...
No wonder tear-drops fall when you call, Northern Ireland,
Northern Ireland, my home.

THE BELFAST BATTLER

A tribute in verse to the memory of Tommy Stewart, former Northern Ireland Flyweight Champion (1938). Born 22nd February 1915. Died 31st March 1964.

Stewart was a tradesman who journeyed in pain
and plied his tough trade on a hostile terrain
where mercy was absent by mutual consent
when fair nature changes to warlike intent.
His workshop a roped square, his corner a school,
where teachers advise as he sits on his stool.
He's filled with ambition, commitment and will
but the strength of the man is his punching and skill,
his courage and cunning, his durable chin,
but above all his total obsession to win.
He learned all he knew in a small York Street gym
from shrewd men who fashioned a style to suit him.
They matched him with others of similar design,
and smiled when the rough diamond started to shine.
Tommy trained hard and his sweat filled the place,
ambition burned high in his heart and his face.
He hoped that his talent would enrich his life,
and provide for a family should he take a wife.
In the year thirty-three, having just turned eighteen,
he made his debut on the North's boxing scene.
Historians differ on whom he first faced
for memories fade and some bouts can't be traced.
Thomas and Finnegan both get the shout
as opponents in his first professional bout.
He beat both these men and had his hand raised,
promoters took note and his prospects were praised.
As that year ended the tally was five

in a trade where the toughest and smartest survive.
In the east-end of Belfast, the Shankill, and Falls,
men fought for a pittance in dank smoky halls,
whilst ruthless promoters who lived off their sweat
would cut to the bone any purse they would get.
Stewart garnered an army of fans with his skill,
crowds flocked to the venues when he topped the bill.
Jack Harvey, Joe Bradley, and Tommy Bodell
all crossed the channel and all quickly fell,
as did Roy Fitsimmons and Lefty McKie
when they shared a ring with this tough Belfast Fly.
They wilt to the pressure of each punch he fires
and he'll punch till his body falls down or expires.
Surrender's a word that is never considered
though some bouts may see him engulfed and embittered.
Though bloody and battered he never will yield,
he'll fight till they carry him out on his shield.
His three fights with Curry were brutal and bruising
for defeat or retreat were not words of his choosing.
But he learns from these bouts and, according to friends,
his schooling pays off, his apprenticeship ends.
Spectators approve with a cascade of sound
when opponents are stretchered and hospital-bound.
Men talk of his courage, his grace in defeat,
he earns his degree in the science that's sweet.
Opponents were out-gunned and quite often decked
as he gathered momentum and gained new respect.
As a time-served technician, he wasn't unnerved,
all rules of engagement were strictly observed.
He mixed with the greatest and in thirty-six,
he met Peter Kane and taught him some new tricks.
For ten hard and fast rounds he stayed there with Kane
as the future world champion tried all night in vain
to land a big punch to put Stewarty away.
The referee stopped it too quickly, friends say.
This could be true, for the newspapers show
the last round had less than two minutes to go.
But everyone called it one helluva bout,
and the York Street man's courage was never in doubt.
Kane was a blacksmith: this caused Stewart to say,
"That guy had a hammer in each hand today."
Manchester, Liverpool, Glasgow, Dundee—
he'd travel wherever he'd get a fair fee.

He'd go anywhere if the money was right
and give away height, weight and reach in a fight.
He fought Jackie Paterson in thirty-eight,
the result was a draw, but the action was great.
Paterson fought his way right to the top,
but always remembered the Tommy Stewart scrap.
From off Corporation Street came a real threat,
at the Oval, one Friday, the near-neighbours met.
Rinty could croon, but he sang dumb that night,
Stewart boxed like a champion and he took the fight.
At the King's Hall return an excitement had grown
for both men were hewed from the same block of stone.
In the peak of condition, fantastically fit,
Monaghan proved he could fight and could hit.
Stewarty went down from a right in Round Two,
but he sprang back at Rinty and hard punches flew.
Young Rinty was schooled in the same sweat-filled joints,
and made it all level when he won on points.
Stewart finished the year fighting good local men,
and met Jim McStravick whom he stopped in ten.
That gave him the coveted North Ireland crown
but he wanted Rinty and hunted him down.

The world was at war when they met once again,
the rubber-match promised excitement and pain.
Both men could punch with considerable force,
and the crowd were surprised when the fight took its course.
The ref lifted Rinty's hand, Stewart paused to say,
"That kid's the best flyweight in this world today."
He wished Rinty luck and he watched him climb high—
fate wasn't as kind to this courageous guy.
For seven hard years he'd fought only the best,
but illness was forcing his brave heart to rest.
With well over one hundred fights to his name,
he stood down in 'forty and gave up the game.
At least three opponents won the world flyweight crown,
his skill took him close, but his luck let him down.
Could anyone blame him for heaving a sigh—
through no fault of his own, the parade had passed by.
Reviews of his fights say no flyweight was tougher,
but his murderous trade left a pain hard to suffer.
He treated this ailment just like a new foe,
and like two contenders they fought toe to toe.

But death was too strong and He won the last round—
the only opponent to keep Tommy down.
The great hands lay stilled in a coffin of pine,
he'd fought his last fight. He was just forty-nine.
York Street was lined as he went to his grave,
the district turned out for the Warrior Brave.
Old boxers who'd faced him quite openly cried
as they tolled the last count for a comrade who'd died.
But his memory will linger when sporting men meet
and talk of the boxer from old Henry Street,
who came close to greatness but missed out on fame—
a champion uncrowned in the world's hardest game.

LISTED BUILDINGS

When I sit down with pals of mine to drink and shoot the breeze,
the atmosphere's relaxing. We argue, sleg and tease.
We talk about the fighting men, the characters, the shrewd ...
(In York Street jargon 'shrewd' translates as local boys made good.)
One day last week we settled in, but soon there was dispute,
as we talked about the Big Buroo and the pubs that sprawled *en route*.

We found it hard to pass them by with our unemployment pay,
although the dough we got then wouldn't buy two pints today.
The argument kept raging till the barman called out 'Time'
that's when I was commissioned to record the bars in rhyme.
"You're settin' me one awful task," I moaned to the clientele,
then I got to thinking about the vanished pubs and was silent for a
                                                              spell.

They should be put in writing, for when we're all dead and gone,
our kids won't know where we spent our time, if we don't pass it on.
I chewed upon this logic and admitted it was true—
those pubs were steeped in history. Our fathers drank there too.
There's no record of these taverns, most of which were bulldozed
                                                              flat,
so I made a solemn promise to immortalise the lot.

But I'd need to get some order, some semblance to the chore,
to put each house in sequence, maybe twenty bars or more.

To appreciate the exercise, I'd need to let you see
the length and breadth of the district and the problems it caused me.
Four streets ran in parallel from the railway to the Co.
(That's the Co-Operative Building for those not in the know.)

Inside those streets were inner streets, some narrow, dark and
                                                                    mean,
they housed some bars where decent types of men would not be seen.
In others foreign seamen mixed with us and drank their fill,
when York Street was a place to be and not a muddy hill.
To cut out any argument, I'd need to set a date,
so I settled for when the rot set in, about nineteen sixty-eight.

And I'd need to state a sad fact: they weren't all knocked down.
Some were blown to pieces, others fire-bombed to the ground.
So I thought I'd start at the L.M.S. and work my way to town,
now I mean that metaphorically, for there's none of them around.
I felt my mind's eye squinting as I put it to the task.
Recalling twenty years ago is an awful lot to ask.

Then came another headache. My heart sank to my feet.
What about the boozers on the far side of the street?
They'd need to be included, the purist in me said,
so I took a large deep breath and ran along them in my head.
Morrison's was The Railway Bar at the corner of Canning Street,
where folk from all round Ireland would find a welcome seat.

The Edinburgh Castle with its nightly cabaret,
then came The Gibraltar. It was next along the way.
Ye Old Castle sat at Spencer Street, I can hear its sing-song still,
at Henry Street The White Lion sat in the shadow of York Street Mill.
Then my mind returned to Whitla Street and made my tired eyes
                                                                    seek
The Waterloo and The Terminus where they both sat cheek to cheek.

Next I stopped at Fleet Street and the well-known Sportsman's
                                                                    Arms,
where we supped our stout and sheltered from the pain of life's
                                                                    alarms.
At Dock Street sat The White Hart Bar, Big Jack Mallon's place,
a coal fire burned in the first box where we sipped at a leisurely pace.
By Trafalgar Street sat The Bowling Green, Paddy Murphy was
                                                                    Mine Host,
over quite a stretch to Little Patrick Street I floated like a ghost.

My final call was The City Arms, that's the York Street list
                                                        complete,
so I made my way to Simon's Bar, which is in Great Patrick Street.
There the two M's ran a sing-song to a packed lounge every night,
in days when life was peaceful and you'd seldom see a fight.
The King's Arms was in Nile Street, two sisters handled things
in a wee bar by the playground everybody called The Swings.

Along Earl Lane was The Regent Bar, a recent change of name,
it used to be The Stalingrade, filled with ladies on the game.
I zoomed by Madgie Walshe's, past King Billy on the wall,
to where Galbraith's Bar at Ship Street was my next port of call.
Along the Lane to Whitla Street, right turn, then right again!
And there sat Barney Vallely's where we dulled our aches and pain.

Down Nelson Street I wandered, past Jack Trainor's pub I sped.
At The Bear's Paw in Great George's Street, I stopped with a sense of
                                                        dread.
I knew something was missing and my head began to spin ...
to my left was Oul Ma Carroll's, on my right The Toddle Inn.
Again into Great Patrick Street my fleshless spirit flew.
Turning left, I almost stopped and signed on the Buroo.

I moved to Corporation Street where The Sunflower used to
                                                        bloom.
At Earl Street sat The Bunch Of Grapes, how we loved its wee
                                                        back room.
The London House at North Thomas Street, with The Magic
                                                        opposite,
From York House down to Benny Coyle's, my restless soul did flit.
Last one left was Cullens, also known as The Dufferin Arms,
it faced the gates to the Pollock Dock where men once toiled
                                                        in swarms.

These houses served a purpose, they quenched the daily thirst
of men who fought the system and always came off worst.
But now those hallowed buildings have vanished without trace,
along with other landmarks that gave the place its grace.
Of course, some pubs still cater for the worker and the tar.
The Dockworkers' Club is in Pilot Street, as is the Rotterdam Bar.

At the bottom of Princes' Dock Street, Pat's friendly light
                                                        still glows,

The American Bar at Short Street, used to be known as Joe's.
I couldn't leave O'Rourke's out, at the corner of Garmoyle Street,
then I doubled back to add Muldoon's which made the list complete.
I spent some time in every house and knew each owner well,
and the anecdotes I've gathered would take a book to tell.

I showed the finished product to my mates the other day.
I know it's not a masterpiece, but it says all I wanted to say.
So I sat down to a well-earned pint as the manuscript was read,
when he'd studied it astutely, one guy looked up and said:
"You've really done a good job. We're well pleased with the text.
Now put your thinkin' cap back on ... You can do the Bookies next!"

THE SAILOR

"Why do yeh go?" I asked my da.
"Why do yeh leave us without ye?
Ma says yeh say it's the call of the sea,
an' ma says she doesn't doubt ye"

"Son, when yiv got the sea in yer blood
an' a yen for those faraway places
Yill turn yer back on the comforts of home
an' yer family's anxious faces.
Yill only feel an affinity when the hawsers rasp an' slide,
an' ya feel her chuggin' away from the quay,
on the breast of the mornin' tide."

"Why do ye leave a safe job on the shore,
for one that is so fraught with dangers?
Why do you flee from the family you love,
to bed down with men who are strangers?
Ma says it's somethin' to do with the tide,
does its ebbin' an' flowin' upset ye?
Ma says it makes you feel restless inside,
an' yeh say yeh must go, an' she lets ye."

"Son, if ye knew of the loneliness,
you'd find my next answer surprisin'.
There's no job onshore that's as hard as the sea,
yet I long for that distant horizon.

Son, can't ye see that my kit-bag is packed,
there's a ship in the harbour that calls me.
There's smoke belchin' outa its salt-crusted stack,
I must board her whatever befalls me."

LAMENT FOR AN ARAB

The Arab, as they were collectively known,
were part of the quay like its concrete and stone.
Along with the seagull, the fish and the rat,
he clung to its belly and lived off its fat.
He off-loaded windjammers, schooners and sloops,
toiled in the bowels of ships of all groups.
Steamer and brigantine, packet and barque,
he carried their cargoes from dawn until dark.
The nickname of Arab was meant to deride,
but he took it and gave it distinction and pride.

Picture his image: the shabby cloth cap,
the confident air or the hesitant step,
the permanent grimace or mischievous grin,
in need of a haircut, or unshaven chin.

From his top jacket pocket peeped a tiny hand-hook,
which went with the Arab on each job he took.
The name of the owner was carved on its end,
for this was his partner, his helper, his friend.

Inside the jacket insurance cards lay,
to be shown at the box where he signed on each day,
except for the odd time a favour was granted,
and he got a job that nobody else wanted.

On mornings when nothing was left for his kind,
he'd make his way down to the dole where he signed,
stood in the queue and just waited his turn.
Time was no object, he'd plenty to burn.
Now and again his bright spirit would sag,
when he hadn't the price of a pint or a fag.
The day loomed before him, each started the same,
hoping the foreman would call out his name.

Through life the same pattern, the pen, the buroo ...
He knew in his heart it was all he could do.
His clothes bore the dust of the last job he'd had,
his lungs held it also. It made him cough bad.
The scars on his skin were from chemical splashes,
some men disguised them with beards and moustaches.
His rough working shirt would be faded and frayed,
just like his jeans and the cap on his head.
Broad braces and belt held his trousers aloft,
the scarf round his neck would be spotted and soft.
He wore heavy boots coloured grey with cement.
Some dockers eyed him with fear and contempt.

His name could be Cochrane, Murphy or Todd,
English or Largey, McMullen or Dodd.
Lyttle or Donaghy, Bailie or Strain,
Marley or Wilson, McNamara ... Cobain.
Thompson or Nelson, McNerlin or Graham,
Crawford or Nesbitt, McAnulty or Frame.

His credentials were guts mixed with desperate need,
he took what was going, his family to feed.
He swept-up in holds filled with dangerous fumes,
and lived in old houses or damp dingy rooms.
Many died young from the pressures and strain
working on quays unprotected from rain,
or inhaling the poison that stifled their breath,
sowing their lungs with the seeds of their death.

He worked at the rosies, the mill or the clay,
hand-walloping cargoes from pallet or tray.
Orange boats, onion boats, timber and flour,
or knee-deep in maize-meal all rancid and sour.

He drank in the Sportsmans', the Bunch or Big Jack's,
Trainor's or Thornton's ... The Alex or Mac's.
The Magic, the Majestic ... The old Bowling Green.
Fisher's or Donnelly's was where he'd be seen.

His lunch would consist of black porter or stew.
At tea-time a snowball or sorehead would do.

He'd get to the pen on a bus or a tram—
if his clothing was dirty they'd tell him to scram.

He was more often seen on a ramshackle bike,
others who lived close enough would just hike.

Once there, he'd stand at the back of the schools,
meekly observing the unwritten rules.
The blues and the reds would divide up the best,
then he and his equals would fight for the rest.
Took on whatever the others refused,
and went home at night often bleeding and bruised.

From the Falls and the Alley they came for a spell,
the Shankill, the Markets ... Greencastle ... Whitewell.
The Bay or the New Lodge, the city's east-end,
the Hammer, the Half-bap, all followed the trend.
The mean streets of Belfast produced him in droves,
they flocked to the pen craving fishes and loaves.

His nickname was Gibby ... Big Wheel ... Double-lap.
Engine or Dekko ... Excitement or Bap.
Bucko or Bandit ... Red-devil or Joker ...
Schemer or Seaspray ... Big Pony or Stoker.
Harloid or Humpy; wee Billy the Rat.
Rainbow and Hairy-Hand ... Sticker and Bat.
Blood-Pressure, Galloper, young Jumpin' Jack,
Winkie and Yella-Hand ... Oul Bacon-neck.

He served in the army, the navy, the skies,
steamed with the convoys and brought back supplies.
Fought in both wars 'cause he thought it was right,
though others stayed out of the Englishman's fight.
He warred in Korea, in Cyprus as well.
When drunk he mourned comrades who lie where they fell.
He lived through mistakes like the Somme and Dunkirk,
came home and had to fight harder for work.

The stevedores used them to break union rules,
the gangers despised them and used them as tools
to upset the dockers, who hated the breed,
ignoring their poorness and desperate need.

If they didn't produce of their best every day,
next morning the foreman would turn them away.
Or else they'd grow old and just couldn't compete,
with the young ones who jostled and tramped on their feet.

Swarming like wildebeast fighting for food,
so the dockers decided to starve out the brood.

Containerisation was the price they would pay
to blot out this stigma and wipe him away.
Mechanisation meant some jobs would go,
but no way could the Arab survive the next blow.
Decasualisation—an infamous day—
when the registered dockers at last got their way.

No compensation was mentioned or given
as out of the sheds and the berths he was driven.
Not one word of protest from union or bosses,
nobody cared for his pain or his losses.
Some men would never again earn a wage,
yet no newspaper mentioned this vicious outrage.
The system that broke him was putrid and rotten,
thrown out like a dog and as quickly forgotten.
He left without rancour, accepted his fate,
went without argument, fuss or debate.

With his exit the hard work went out of the game.
All they do now is put hooks in a frame,
The crane or the lift-truck will take and supply,
the whole exercise could be done by one guy.

No more do they shoulder rough sacks till they bleed,
top up the 'tween-decks or follow the lead.
Sling hot cement in the glare of the sun,
truck tons of slag with a galloping run.
No staggering home to pour urine on blisters ...
The work nowadays could be done by their sisters.

These were the Arabs who toiled at the tide,
used and exploited then tossed to the side.
Stamped on like insects by men with no shame ...
All that remains is their much maligned name ... Arab.
    Arab, I Salute You.

SONG OF A SON OF THE OLD SCHOOL

The squad was sat in Barney's snug, relaxin' in the heat.
A blizzard lashed the windies an' the hot rum tasted sweet.
We'd bin rained-off at a timber-boat, an' our backs
        were strained and sore,
slingin' lengths of Oregon pine stretchin' forty feet or more.
All that week we'd struggled with nipper chains an' wires,
whilst dodgin' drunken winchmen an' avoidin' butts an' flyers.
We gabbled through each other, talkin' heel-sticks, hooks an' straps,
till an oul lad in the corner snarled, "Will yis shut yer bloody traps".

He pushed his well-worn cap back an' scratched his silver head,
glarin' round the loose-box, with a scornful sneer he brayed:
"That timber-boat's a bloody gift—yev a winch for Heaven's sake.
We shouldered bales from ship to shore all day without a break.
An' we didn't start at eight o'clock an' stop at half-past-five.
We worked from dawn 'til dusk those days. There was no
        such word as skive.
The ganger stalked the 'tween-decks. All day he give us hell,
then waited with his hand out for a kick-back from yer spell.

"We worked through rain an' blizzards like the one
        that's blowin' now.
There was no such thing as unions to fight the men in power.
With eyes burnt red by sawdust, we humped the twelve-by-threes.
Sometimes the weight of a rain-soaked plank wud force us
        to our knees.
When daylight went we'd stumble blind across an unlit deck.
Some men wud slip an' pray to God they hadn't broke their back.
But he had to rise up pronto an' get back in the race,
or they'd get another fella to take his bloody place.

"Our blistered shoulders took the brunt of every coarse-cut plank.
Despite the coul we'd sweat like pigs 'til everybody stank.
But each heart dreamed of quittin' time an' a drink in a quiet place
away from the screams of the ganger an' the pain of
        the back-breakin' pace.
When I was young the men were steel an' the ships were
        bloody wood.
We didn't take a dinner-break 'cause we cudn't buy the food.
I was eighty-three last weekend an' my anchor's nearly weighed,
but I'd still be a better man than youse if I was six months dead.

So leave the timber in the hatch. Stop slingin' in the snug.
The guy who mentions work again is the guy I'm gonna slug."
A quietness descended; we looked out at the rain.
Except to order more hot rums, we didn't speak again.

THERE ARE MEN LIKE THAT

There are men like that when trouble advances,
they'll charge a cannon with broken lances,
to engage the injustice that eternally springs.
There are men abroad who would do such things.

There are men like that who'll face the flak,
use their God-given right to stand up and talk back,
fight unequal odds to the final bell,
take their blood-stained virtue to the gates of hell.

There are men like that in this world today
who would take an issue like that all the way.
They'll scorn the danger such a move entails
and ride it to victory, or off the rails.

There are men like that who won't run away
when the vultures gather and the jackals bay.
Filled with compassion, fired by its flame.
They'll plead for the humble, or die in their name.

There are men like that who will not bend the knee,
who will risk all they own to defend you and me.
Principled men, men of courage and mettle
who'll bite the hot bullet and grasp the sharp nettle.

There are men like that and, from cradle to grave,
they'll oppose every effort to make you a slave.
Quiet men of valour, with manners unassuming,
they'll stand at your side when a crisis is looming.

There are men such as that. They could live in your street.
Men who refuse to be broken or beat.
Should you chance to meet one, give his back a good pat,
then thank God in Heaven, there is still men like that!

I CARE FOR THE PEOPLE

I care for the people, the poor and the needy,
exploited and used by the rich and the greedy.
Forever downtrodden by power and rank,
kept on their knees by the boss and the bank.

I care for the people, bewildered and sad,
slaving in jobs where conditions are bad.
Dead-end positions that stifle and stun,
whilst promotion's reserved for the manager's son.

I care for the people; how can they save,
existing on hand-outs from cradle to grave?
Watching their children passed over, ignored,
craving possessions they just can't afford.

I care for the people and long for the hour
they cast off their shackles and blossom and flower,
and join in the fight to live equal and free,
without touching forelocks and bending the knee.

OLD SOLDIER

He went with the Rifles to Europe.
When the nightmare of warfare began,
a voice from within softly whispered:
"You'll survive this and die an old man."
It started when he left the Shankill
and stayed with him through World War II.
As he soldiered in mud, flood and furnace,
he hoped what the voice said was true.

As men fell in battle all round him,
he went where his officer led,
doing the job he signed on for,
and homesick for his little bed.
For bed is the safest of places,
it cocooned him from everything bad.
He longed to lie under its blankets,
within earshot of mother and dad.

He fought through the minefields and craters,
where comrades lay dying or dead.
As tracer-fire raked all around him,
the voice said: "You'll die in your bed."
He advanced through the heat of each battle,
as star-shells burst over his head,
Snatching some sleep in a shell-hole—
if no one was watching, he prayed.

Though the horror of war filled his ear-drums,
he believed the small voice as it said:
"You'll live through this death and destruction,
and die in your own little bed."
And that's where he died in his old age,
a victim of treacherous chance,
in a Belfast as vicious and deadly,
as a foxhole in occupied France.

He was murdered by human excreta,
who committed the ultimate crime.
Bludgeoned to death the old soldier,
and then crawled back into the slime.
His blood and his flesh stained the blankets,
as mercy and tolerance fled.
The voice had been right when it whispered:
"You'll die an old man in your bed."

THE OLD MAN AND THE SOVEREIGNS
A short story in verse

I was stannin' in Barney's one evenin', suppin' a bottle or two,
wilin' away a few hours. I'd nuthin' much better to do.
An oul fella, stannin' beside me, stared deeply into his glass,
his wee body still as a statue, his face hard and set like a mask.
I cudn't contain it much longer. I shouted, "Hi Barney, two stout,"
then turned to the sad-faced oul fella. If I waited, he'd soon
    spit it out.
His sad grey eyes turned and luked at me. He said, "I can't
    buy you one back."
I answered, "That don't make a matter. Sit down, givus some
    of yer crack.

"I kin tell by yer voice yer not local, from where in the world do
     you hail?"
He sipped at the Guinness and whimpered, "I'm just outa Townhall
     Street Jail.
I was lifted last night by the peelers and tossed in that dirty oul clink.
I'm as sick as a sow having piglets and badly in need of this drink."
I nodded my head as he thanked me. I said, "What's that accent
     you own?"
The sad grey eyes gladdened a little as he whispered, "It's County
     Tyrone.
County Tyrone with its mountains, its forests and meadows so fair.
County Tyrone my sweet homeland. Oh God, how I wish I was there.

"I wus hired to a farm near Dungannon for all of my long
     working life.
I slept in the barn with the livestock, and never found time for a wife.
I toiled from the dawn till the darkness and never knew smokin'
     or beer.
I wus fed by my master and mistress, and paid one gold sovereign
     a year."
He paused as I rose from the table an' ordered another two stout.
His eyes gleamed with anticipation as slowly he poured the drink
     out.
"One sovereign a year," I repeated, "for workin' from morning
     to night?
I'm not a great mathematician, but somehow that doesn't
     soun' right."

He gazed in his glass and smiled vaguely. I sensed he was back
     in Tyrone,
walkin' the fields an' the forests, so I shut up an' left him alone.
Some moments later he shuddered an' emptied his glass with a sigh.
"I'm leaving, so thanks for your kindness, but I won't drink unless I
     can buy."
"Ack, stay for a wee while," I pleaded, "shure another won't do ye
     no harm.
I'm dyin' to know all about ye. Tell me, when did ye leave
     the oul farm?"
"Yesterday morning," he muttered. "I'd been there for sixty-five
     years.
I left with my sixty-five sovereigns, and came to this valley of tears.

"I boarded a train bound for Belfast, a town I'd long hankered
     to see.

I thought of the things I wud do there, now I was wealthy and free.
I went to a pub called Dubarry's and tasted my first drop of drink.
Whilst there I met a sweet maiden, whose loveliness caused me
    to blink.
I blushed when she said, 'Hiya, honey,' and hooked herself
    onto my arm,
adding 'Where have you been all my life boy?' and I answered
    'Down on the farm.'
The barman examined the sovereign I'd give him to pay for the beer.
I said, 'If that isn't sufficient, don't worry, I've plenty more here.'

The girl wrapped her lovely arms round me, and asked me to take
    her outside—
she wanted to walk in the moonlight with a fine looking man
    at her side.
I woke in the back of a police car. Two cops held me down
    with their feet.
They tole the big sarge in the barrack they found me dead drunk
    in the street.
They tossed me out early this morning, and called me a drunken
    oul lout.
That's why I cried at your kindness when you bought me them
    bottles of stout.
That Jezebel stole all my sovereigns, took all the money I own.
I'm lost and alone in a city, a long way from County Tyrone."

He sat in a daze at the table, wracked by self-pity an' doubt.
I borrowed the dough for his fare home an' bought some more
    bottles of stout.
When he stud up to leave some hours later, I rose up an' offered
    my han'.
They'd stolen his pride an' his money an' left him a heartbroken
    man.
A tired smile crossed his pale features. "I know I'm a silly oul fool,
but the last time I walked with a female, I was taking a cow
    to the bull.
I'm more used to draining out peat bogs and quenching my thirst
    at a brook,
or watching the dawn light the forest from my bed in a warm
    hay-filled nook."

He slouched to the door of the bar-room, his eyes glazed, his jaw
    limp an' slack.

I shouted, "Ack, come on oul fella, mopin' won't bring yer dough
    back."
He flashed me a smile of defiance, yet somehow he made my tears
    flow
when he said in a voice tinged with sadness; "Ack well. Easy come,
    easy go."

BIG AL

Big Al: denim clad,
    possessed by a habit that drives him mad
    and sends him off on gigantic binges,
    that blows his mind to the outer fringes.

Big Al: shipyard steel,
    until his cover begins to peel.
    Then insecurity pulls up a chair
    and is manifested in his wall-eyed stare.

Big Al: when the phantoms call,
    he bounces the music from wall to wall.
    The mega blast brings a hearing risk
    as he sings along with a compact disc.

Big Al: twilight zones,
    duets all night with the Rolling Stones.
    When the party's over he wakes up shaking,
    his flag half-mast and his paintwork flaking.

Big Al: simply great
    if you get him at his best-by date.
    Before he imbibes the alcohol vapours
    that make him indulge in despicable capers.

Big Al: colour him bad
    as Peter Pan mimics Jack the lad.
    Drunken mountebank. Foul-mouthed jerk.
    The prototype of a nasty piece of work.

Big Al: enigma rare,
    flies gutter-low on the wings of despair,

as vaguely-remembered bouts with disgrace
adds one more furrow to his guilt-lined face.

Big Al: when the ghosts appear,
  he clings to the music that quells his fear.
Like mother's milk it brings content
  to a tortured soul that seems hell-bent.

Big Al: prematurely grey,
  he battles his demons day by day.
Sometimes alone in a darkened room
where imagined horrors chill a pitiless gloom.

Big Al: dreads the hovering wings
  of the vicious circle each new day brings.
On every corner the spectres lurk ...
and fighting devils can be thirsty work.
  Good luck, Big Al.

IT DIDN'T HURT
A true incident in verse

It didn't hurt when they beat me with the weapons
or when they smashed my nose and broke my jaw.
It didn't hurt when they kicked my helpless body.
It only hurt when her tear-stained face I saw.

It didn't hurt when the doctor stitched my head-wounds.
It didn't hurt when they jabbed me for the pain.
It didn't hurt when they filled my arm with needles,
but it hurt to know I'd hurted her again.

It didn't hurt in the operating theatre,
though they worked on me for an hour and a half.
It hurt to know that once again I'd hurt her
and made her cry more times than I'd made her laugh.

It didn't hurt when I woke from the operation,
though my body ached and my face was wracked with pain.
It didn't hurt when my jaw was strapped and wired.
It hurt because her prayers were all in vain.

It didn't hurt when they wouldn't give me water
or medicine to ease a throat so dry.
It only hurt when I looked into her sad eyes,
and it hurt me bad when I saw her start to cry.

THE RHYMING POET AT WORK

The seeds of a theme begin to germinate,
juggling perception with space and time,
distilling a literary concentrate,
whilst weaving a web of words in rhyme.

Spare with verbiage, he'll favour not
a word, because it seems to fit.
For the precise word in its proper slot
can produce a pattern for the verse to knit.

Uniting intellect with soul and brain,
these faculties he'll utilise.
The servile words will sense his pain,
perfection seeking compromise.

A word-processor might speed his quest,
a rhyming dictionary aid the cause,
but the finished product will not be blessed
with the gratification of self-applause.

Checking the syntax for structured strength,
he'll measure the metre for span of life,
count each serving syllable's length
whilst marrying stanzas like man and wife.

He'll reassess each chosen word,
or eliminate it with a pencil stroke.
It's akin to snaring an extinct bird,
or creating substance from a puff of smoke.

A DEATH IN THE AFTERNOON

He was old and fat and overweight and struggled hard for breath,
unaware, until the last minute, that I'd set him up for death.
He was bored and voiced that opinion, every dawn he whined
    to be free.
I reckoned if I didn't kill him, then the son-of-a-bitch would kill me.

Yet he was my pal on the lonely nights when nobody wanted to know.
His loyalty went unquestioned, but one of us had to go.
We dandered the last mile together. When he looked up at me
    I just smiled,
yet my conscience was giving me trouble: I felt I was killing a child.

But he never suspected betrayal as he waddled along at my side.
I'd planned his demise just that morning. I was taking my pal
    for a ride.
An assassin was waiting to kill him. I'd set-up the time and the place.
He entered where he would be murdered with nothing
    but trust in his face.

He was puzzled when struck by the first blow, a sly subtle jab
    in his side.
I searched his sad eyes for forgiveness as he lay where so many
    had died.
The minutes ticked by as I waited, wondering if I'd done right.
The assassin demanded his money, my pal slowly lost his last fight.

I thought of the first time I saw him, when into our family he came.
We promised to love and protect him. How can I live with
    this shame?
His assassin delivered the last blow, he departed with one final
    breath.
I rose from his side feeling humbled, distressed by the vision
    of death.

My old friend had trusted me deeply. The guilt cut my heart
    like a knife.
My pettiness brought on the judgement—disturbing my sleep
    meant his life.
Now I sit like a man in bereavement. His departure has left
    a great gap.
No more will I slip him a tit-bit, or give his broad back a fond slap.

I hope he has gone somewhere pleasant, with plenty of room
    to explore,
where he can run free and unfettered, and feel like a young pup
    once more.
The vet said, "You'll soon get another", as he reached me his collar
    and lead.
I left my dead pal on the cold floor, praying Prince would forgive
    my vile deed.

I'M IN LOVE WITH A RADIO DEEJAY

I'm in love with a radio deejay and live for the sound of her voice,
as she talks about listeners' problems and plays them the songs
    of their choice.
I sit by my little transistor, lost in a dream all the while,
pretending she's right there beside me, lighting my world
    with her smile.
I get just a little bit jealous when she interviews men of esteem
like singers and authors and actors. I imagine she makes their
    eyes gleam.
I'm not in the least bit creative, but she brings out the poet in me.
I've written her hundreds of sonnets, she's all I would wish her to be.
I saw her one day down in Bangor, she was opening up a new store.
Mobbed by the fans who adore her, she signed autographs
    by the score.
I savoured her beauty all morning, though I'm not a celebrity freak.
When she smiled in my general direction, I was over the moon
    for a week.
One time I sent a request in, for a girl with a similar name,
and asked her to play a sweet love song for the lady, who was
    an old flame.
She read out the whole dedication, not knowing each word was
    for her.
"Honey, this guy really loves you," she laughed with a sensual purr.
I'm in love with a radio deejay, but it's unrequited my friends ...
for the lady is happily married, so I'll nurse this old heart till
    it mends.

SOUNDS THAT GIVE ME PLEASURE

Frank Sinatra singing 'Laura',
Tony Bennet singing 'Till',
Johnny Mathis singing 'Misty',
Helen Morgan singing 'Bill'.

Perry Como's 'Magic Moments',
Dinah Washington with 'Wrong',
Peggy Lee performing 'Fever',
Nat King Cole's 'September Song'.

'Good Vibrations' by the Beach Boys,
'Satisfaction' by the Stones,
'Penny Lane' sung by the Beatles,
'Can't Get Started' by Jack Jones.

'When the World was Young' by Crosby,
'Pretty Woman' by Big O,
Don Maclean with 'Crying',
The Four Freshmen with 'Speak Low'.

Jolson singing 'Swanee',
Dionne Warwick's 'Walk On By'.
Gerry Vale performing 'Linda',
The Four Aces 'Tell Me Why?'

These are sounds that
bring me pleasure
every time I hear them play.
They transport me through
the seasons,
in a pleasant charming way.

THE LECTURE
for Joanne

On her pert little face mischief mingles with grace
when I make her stand still for a lecture.
As she silently listened, a crystal tear glistened,

and slid down her skin of fine texture.
Whilst I loudly upbraided, her features paraded
a gamut of sorrow and grief.
Now and then though, in her soft eyes would glow
a shimmer of shy disbelief.
She listened intently, then promised me gently
with features devout as a saint,
She would go to bed early, stop being surly
and give mum no cause for complaint.
As I threatened and glowered, she shyly stepped forward
and gave me a hug and a kiss.
Mum rolled her eyes, wasn't one bit surprised,
she knew each lecture ended like this.
But I wouldn't be bought, though her searching eyes sought
an end to my blathering bleats.
But after the rocket, I dipped in my pocket
and gave her the dough for some sweets.

MY GIRL
for Barbara

My girl never wore a wedding dress,
she had to settle for a whole lot less.
No big church wedding made her dream complete,
we took our vows in Victoria Street.
Our guest list numbered only three:
they were Ned MacArthur, my da-in-law to be,
my brother Tommy and Eleanor his wife.
They witnessed the start of our married life.

In Tommy's Mini we drove to town,
fed the parking meter with half-a-crown.
The registry office wasn't too far
from Rosemary Street where we parked the car.
The official in charge was a slight, bald guy
in a sombre suit and old school tie.
With a cultured accent he performed the service.
As she held my hand, Barbara seemed quite nervous.

We walked to the Ashley for photographs
and managed to stifle our giggles and laughs,

when they made us pose among wedding fixtures—
my brown hush-puppys spoiled all the pictures.
No large crowds gathered outside the place,
no rice or confetti was thrown in her face,
no waiting chauffeur in a bridal car,
just the wee red Mini, to the Sportsmans' Bar.

Barney set up the first round free
and proposed good health to the bride and me.
Her da seemed pensive throughout the drinking—
I'd a fair idea what he might be thinking.
I'll swear as he sipped from my mum's best delph,
in his new son-in-law, he saw an image of himself.
Just a wayward boozer from a rowdy lot.
I couldn't blame the man for wanting more than that.

We stayed in Barney's 'til he closed the door,
then staggered to our house to drink some more.
In my ma's wee kitchen, by a roaring fire,
we yarned and sang for another hour.
About one in the morning I started to yawn,
but her da held back when the others had gone
His eyes were misty as he gazed at my bride,
then he held her tightly, and he quietly cried.

He turned when he reached the top of Earl Street.
His farewell wave seemed a gesture of defeat.
With his head held low like a funeral mourner,
he disappeared round the bank's grey corner.
I closed the front door and quietly led
the way upstairs to our marital bed,
in the returning room by darkness hid.
Mum bought it in Strongs for about twelve quid.

Right from the start of our married life
my girl remained a most dutiful wife,
whilst I thrashed around in a mire of my making,
not one bit worried that her heart was breaking.
More than once the frail merger cracked
when I bartered dignity and self-respect.
Ignoring my behaviour when I hit the skids,
she filled up the void with our home and our kids.

That's how it happened and those are the facts.
I won't paper over the faults or the cracks
and though there's been many a heartache and tear,
it's growing stronger with each passing year.
My girl didn't get a bridal gown
or a honeymoon in a foreign town—
just a drive in a Mini, a drink in a snug,
and tears from her dad, when he gave her a hug.

JONATHAN
to celebrate his third birthday

He pauses a while in the doorway,
with a smile of disarming affection.
Then a mischievious grin lights his features,
and he charges in my direction.
As I gather him up in my welcoming arms
I wait for his first request.
"Football!" he orders and narrows his eyes,
till I rise from my pre-dinner rest.
We head for the back-garden, hand in hand,
and spend some time kicking a ball.
I laugh as he gallops and giggles and leaps,
and shudder when he takes a fall.
He'll climb up the oil-tank or jump off a ledge,
when naughty, he'll throw the ball over the hedge.
The first time he did this I ordered him in.
His eyes filled with tears, and he then kicked my shin.
Regretting my outburst, I signalled a truce,
and we went to the kitchen and drank orange juice.
We then ate some apples. He glowed with content.
Hours like these are the nicest I've spent.
It's a glorious feeling, well nurtured by pride
when a man and his first grandson sit side by side.
To this little infant, life's only a game,
and I think of the time when his dad was the same.
But we tire of this nonsense, and take a short hike
to Granda's wee room and his exercise bike.
He'll clamber up on it, just like the big boys,
then he'll switch on the console and yell: "What's that noise?"

And he'll laugh as I frantically search for the sound.
It's a game we play every time he comes around.
When his dad says "C'mon boy", the way dads command,
I solemnly reach out and shake his wee hand.
No way would I kiss him for we would both blush.
His grandmothers do it. They're into that mush.
I went to my granda's when I was his age,
but my memory only turns up a blank page.
I'm recording these moments for, as years unfold,
they may fade from the mind of a boy three years old,
but now they're recounted and transcribed in ink.
When he plays with his grandson, he may sense the link
with the old man who sat with him sharing his joys
when we played on the carpet like two little boys.
I hope he remembers and pray that it's so,
when this day takes its leave and becomes long ago.

LOUISE AND I

The time flies by when Louise and I,
sit down for a little talk.
This chatterbox is as cute as a fox,
and endowed with the eyes of a hawk.
And although she's only three, she asks questions
that would baffle better men than me!
"Why does the snow melt and go when the sun is warm?
Why do leaves get blown from the trees by a storm?"
And on and on it goes. "Granda, who lights the stars up,
and who puts the petals on a rose?"

As I search for replies, she'll look deep in my eyes,
"Granda why is your hair going grey?
Granny tells me you're wise, and you never tell lies ...
Granda, where are we going today? And why can't I drink beer?
And why does my birthday only come once a year?"
And on and on it goes. "Granda, who lights the stars up,
and who puts the petals on a rose?"

When we sit down to tea still the questions hit me.
"Granda, why can't I drive your car? Is Santa Claus tall?
Will he bring me a ball? Does he live on the moon or a star?"

When she's ready for bed, questions still fill her head.
"Granda, why is it little boys fight? and where does Johnny Dark
go, when you turn on the bedroom light?"
The questions she asks are the ones you expected least.
"Granda, who is the Sandman, and why did Beauty love the Beast?"
And on and on and on till sweet repose. "Granda, who lights
   the stars up,
and who puts the petals on a rose?"

from
SATURDAY NIGHT IN YORK STREET
(1982)

FIVE SHORT POEMS

The Place
"Sailorstown, is this it?" said the young lad to his dad.
"Stretching all around you," said the father to his lad.
"It's the greatest district. Finer people you won't meet."
"Ack, Da," said the wee buck, "all I see's a dirty street."

The People
Buck Alec, Rinty Monaghan, James Galway, Gerry Fitt.
All are first-class York Street men with talent, strength and grit.

The Work
Slingin' cement on a hot summer's day,
was like an excursion to Hell they say.
Blinded, melting, caked and tired.
One complaint and you'd get fired.

The Fights
It's said aggression in their hearts
was difficult to smother,
and if a stranger wouldn't fight
they'd set upon each other.
But malice never reigned too long,
they'd meet to slake their thirst,
and try to figure out the bout,
and who hit who the first.

The Troubles
"I'm sorry for your troubles,"
said the Catholic to the Prod.
"Aye," replied his counterpart,
"it's just the work of God.
Someday He may tell us
when our life is done
why we shot your brother
and why youse killed my son."

THE DARK BAD DAYS

The dark bad days are here again,
once more the bards will lay acclaim
to men who take the lives of men.
The dark bad days are here again.

Insidious peace will not prevail,
whilst reforms crawl like a bloated snail
and men are whipped by passion's flame.
The dark bad days are here again.

The spoken word can culminate,
permeate a frenzy black with hate,
and slip the leash of death and pain.
The dark bad days are here again.

If again the bullets sing,
who will gain from this sad thing?
Words just hurt, but bullets maim.
The dark bad days are here again.

When the blood of men has bled,
when we crawl forth to count the dead,
will they all have died in vain?
The dark bad days are here again.

November 1968

CASUAL CURSES

Did you ever sign on the bloody buroo, the bloody buroo,
      the bloody buroo?
You stan' for hours in a big long queue in the bloody buroo
      in Belfast.
Did you ever sign on the casual box, the casual box, the casual box?
They say them lads take some hard knocks on the casual box
      in Belfast.

They make you sign there every day, every day, every day, an' stop
      yer dole if you go astray,
on the casual box in Belfast.

Report for work at eight o'clock, eight o'clock, eight o'clock,
    but there's no bloody
Work on the Belfast Dock for the casual man in Belfast.

They'll starve yer kids on the word of a jerk, word of a jerk,
    word of a jerk,
who say you didn't turn out for work, on the casual box in Belfast.
The way they look when they pay out yer dockets, pay out
    yer dockets, pay out yer dockets,
You'd think it was outa their own bloody pockets ...
in the bloody buroo in Belfast.

I hope to God when my life is through, life is through, life is
    through,
where I go they won't have any bloody buroo, like the bloody buroo
    in Belfast.

JACK

Jack drank the last of his bitter brew and gazed around the motley
    crew
in donkey-jackets, quaffing beer. His scornful smile turned
    to a sneer.
He listened to their petty talk and likened it to chicken-squawk.
He watched their faces work with drink and heard their porter
    tumblers clink,
and knew he hated everyone, each mother's boy and father's son.
He spat with venom on the floor and eyed the drinking men
    once more.
He eyed young Jimmy boozing well, who now and then a tale
    would tell
of knocking some girl up the pole, whilst Andy Black would curse
    his soul,
for Andy Black had daughters ten, he tried to keep from horny men.
But three had finished nursing kids and near put Andy on the skids,
as he was drunk for weeks on end, and cried because he couldn't
    fend.
He swore at Bell and said, "You rats do everything but raise the brats
you like to breed so bloody free. They're born, and reared by mugs
    like me

who'd never show their girls the door, but keep them even though
    they whore."
His crabit face was lined and grey. A man who'd seen a bitter day.
And people smirked behind their hand because he couldn't hold
    command
of daughters beautiful and gay. He lived in dread from day to day.

Jack's face lifted from the men and travelled round the pub again,
filled by laughing, swearing souls, its heat was made from blazing
    coals.
The ceiling was a dingy grey, its paint-work peeled and scraped away.
Its tables, reeking porter stale, were bought, some say, at pauper's
    sale.
Its windows blocked from light of day. No wash for them from May
    to May.

He was jagged to life by a glassy clink as Andy set him up a drink.
Jack glared at him, his face a mask. "I want no drink. I didn't ask."
For in that bar it well was known, Jack Murphy liked to drink alone.
Sour. Dogmatic in his beer, a villain with a built-in sneer.
"You bloody fool! What do you think? You think I'm in here
    bummin' drink?"
Old Andy cringed at this attack. In truth, he was afraid of Jack—
as was each man who drank inside that pub so near the dock's
    black tide.
For Jack was heavy, wide and tall, and harder than the pub's
    brick wall,
and meaner than a dog in pup, who maimed with pleasure
    when worked-up.

The sailor sprawling by the fire could testify to Big Jack's ire.
As could the docker drinking gin, for Jack had beat the hide off him.
The only crime for that attack was that he'd bandied words with Jack.
And Jack soured after a drink or two and kicked the dockie
    black and blue.
The sailor too had learned his lesson. He'd crossed Big Jack and fell
    like Nelson.

Billy Wilde, who owned the House, stood as quiet as a mouse,
and studied well the frightened men who muttered, "Big Jack's
    off again."
Or "God I'm glad I'm not the guy who's found ill-favour in his eye."
Or "Hope he doesn't hurt him much. Old Andy isn't bad as such.
He only tried to buy him ale. I hope he lives to tell the tale."

Fear was bright in Andy's eyes as vainly he apologised,
but Big Jack grabbed him by the throat and ripped the stitching
   in his coat.
And snarled, "You lie, you bloody rat." He eyed the drink. "You
   ordered that.
Don't try to say it's not for me, you dirty stinking little flea."

Young Jimmy Bell cried, "Please don't, Jack. You know oul Andy
   can't fight back.
For Heaven's sake a man like you would break that poor oul fool
   in two.
He's sorry Jack, he didn't think. We know it's just your own
   you drink."
"Shut up," snarled Jack "or you I'll brain" and Jimmy didn't
   speak again.
And Jack retained his vice-like grip, and then he snorted, "Come boy
   ... sit".
And Andy squatted like a dog, and then Jack said, "Croak like
   a frog."
And Andy cried and croaked and sat, whilst Jack roared, "Now boys,
   what of that?"
But all the men felt small as flies, for no man there was Big Jack's
   size.
So Jack continued on the track of bullying old Andy Black.
He sneered at Andy: "Guess you'll know about the time I met
   your Flo.
You know, the one who isn't right. The one whose blue eyes shine
   so bright,
who fills each pretty dress she wears with breasts that hang like young
   fresh pears.
She's kinda looney, that may be, but boys she seemed alright to me.
I saw her sunning in the park and touched her face just for a lark.
Her face was beautiful to see—the stupid bitch gave all to me.
So call me now a stinking rat—I took advantage of your brat."

Old Andy blanched upon the floor, it seemed he couldn't take
   much more.
His face grew red, his lips were curled and filthy oaths at Jack
   he hurled.
"My simple Flo I thought secure from rats like you who'd make
   a whore
of girls who want no art or part, I'll have your black-enamelled
   heart."

And from his coat he drew a knife and rushed at Jack to take his life.
The drinkers scattered from the scene, but Jack remained. His eyes
    were keen.
His knuckles caught the old man's head and Andy fell like he
    was dead,
and sprawling on his open knife, he bled the last of his sad life.
But Jack was neither shocked nor sad. He only said. "Too bad.
    Too bad.
He should have knowed I only joked him, still it wasn't me who
    croaked him."
Judge said same, but cautioned Jack and stated he provoked attack,
and said, "In duty I would fail, if I did not send you to jail."
So three years hard was Jack's reward for helping Andy meet
    the Lord.

Jack had no kin, no friend to say, "I'll visit you on open day."
He sat in woe resigned to rot within the hated prison plot.
He cursed the warden, cursed the screw and yelled, "I'll torment
    all of you."
He'd toss his food across the cell and night by night he'd scream
    and yell.
At exercise Big Man McKimm took him aside and chastised him.
He said, "It's sick the way you wail." (Big Man was kingpin in
    the jail.)
"You've copped a sentence that will stan', so try an' face it like
    a man."
Big Jack's left hand sunk in his gut. His right hand travelled
    half-a-fut.
McKimm woke up in patch-up wing and he remembered not a thing.
But at next exercise in yard, Big Jack was reckoned prison-hard,
and he took over from McKimm, although the inmates hated him.

One day the warder shouted through the peep-hole. "Visitor for you.
Stand to your door, I'll let you out, best promise not to scream
    or shout."
The big man gasped, yet did agree, said, "Who in God would
    visit me?"
He sat as quiet as a pup until his visitor showed up.
He half-expected some old foe, but felt surprise when he saw Flo,
the same sweet Flo he'd met in the park. He nodded at the warder's
    bark:
"No kissing, touching, holding hands, just talking; that the law
    commands."

But lovely Flo was deaf and dumb and from her lips no words
    would come.
Her fragile face was soft with smile and threw Jack's memory back
    a while,
to when he loved her in the park, for once he felt compassion's
    spark.
Within a heart that waxed obscene, he thought he felt a pity wean.
She touched his hand and stroked it soft. The warder soared
    his eyes aloft.
But Big Jack couldn't understand: he'd killed her pa; she held
    his hand.

Although she couldn't say a word, a strange enchanting
    thing occurred.
A wistful smile of gentle grace shone from her eyes onto his face,
and drew the hate and fight from him, and made his past life
    fade and dim.
His hungry eyes ate at her form and in his head the memories
    swarm,
and yet the bad thoughts he won't think and she to him becomes
    life's link.
And as the long years roll away, she visits him each open day.
And brings him cakes and holds his hands, and all the while he
    states his plans.
"Since you came here I've changed my tune. The warden says you've
    been a boon.
He hopes you'll always fill my booth and so do I Flo—that's the
    truth."

Sometimes he thought about that night when she gave in without
    a fight.
To her there was no right or wrong. Oh God, the memory lingered
    long.
He'd savaged her to pain and shame—in the park with lust he'd
    been insane.
His love was savage, brutal, vile, yet sweet Flo never lost her smile.
"By God, I've been a pig to you. I wish to Him I could undo
the wrong I did to you that day. Oh please forgive me Flo, I pray.
I love you girl. I'd give my arm if I could just undo the harm
I did to you those years ago. Oh God. Oh God, forgive me Flo."

He'd cry sometimes, just like a child, as sweet Flo held his hand
    and smiled.
The years went slowly by, as Jack no more the warders did attack.
In fact, he led a model life and planned to make sweet Flo his wife.

He told the guv'nor of his plan and gained respect from screw
    and man.
And every open day came Flo to smile at Jack who loved her so.

He dreamed of how his life would be, next year, when they would
    set him free.
He'd marry Flo and care for her and never make life bare for her.
He'd get a job and mend his way, and love her more with every day.
The change in him was great, they say.   ❧

Then came red-letter day for him. He shook the hand of
    Big McKimm,
and bid the warden warm farewell, no more would he in prison
    dwell.
And Flo stood outside prison gate on that auspicious day and date,
till Jack ducked through the little door and held her in his arms
    once more.
But this time lust was not the cause, he loved her now for what
    she was.
A pretty orphan, kind and mild, a woman who was still a child.
He'd learned to talk to her with hands, and so they chatted
    of their plans.
He held her tight and side by side, they reached the pub close
    to the tide.
Flo entered first, then Jack came through grinning broadly at the
    folk he knew.
He yelled, "Don't fret, I'm turnin' nice an' sweet. Flo's gonna be
    my wife.
Hush now." His big harsh voice commands, "She's talkin' to me
    with her hands."
They watched her spin the mental braille and saw his face turn
    shocked and pale.
And faster than the eye could note, her right hand flashed across
    his throat.
He thudded down like big tree felled. "She's cut his bloody throat,"
    they yelled.

Looking up, his eyes were pained, as from his neck the life-blood
    drained.
It whooshed from vein like garden hose, and saturated sweet Flo's
    clothes.
He cried, "Give me one last embrace." She smiled, and spat down
    on his face,

and with her eyes she drank the toast that down in Hell his soul
   would roast,
and made it plain that daughters ten had someone to look
   after them.

They saw the knife that sliced his throat was that which Andy
   brought from his coat.
The day they picked him from the ground, the pocket knife could
   not be found.
As police searched for it far and near, some said 'twas stole
   as souvenir.
And how it got in hands of Flo was something only she could know.

Then Bill Wilde spoke. His voice cracked low. He rasped, "I'm glad
   to see him go.
For all his life, he's plagued my pub, a dirty rotten ill-reared cub
who took from all and give to noan, except a broken neck or bone
with boot and fist and bloody head. Because of him her father's
   dead."
He glared at those within his view and snarled, "I'm warnin' each
   of you—
Jack Murphy's dead and I'll swear free, that bloody thug was killed
   by me."

For moments rare a silence hung, then Docker said, "Bill, hold
   yer tongue.
Shure any half-eyed fool cud see that imp of hell was knifed by me."
The knife was cleaned of fingerprint and every man-jack did
   his stint.
"I stabbed the bastard," Sailor cried, "although I'm sad the way
   he died."
Young Jimmy yelled, "Go swab the deck. You're tellin' lies. I killed
   Big Jack."

When questions by the cop began, he got this story from each man.
"I killed the bastard. I croaked him. I made his light of life go dim."
They yelled in unison at the cop, "I stuck the pig, I made him drop."
And someone said, "The others lie, for I'm the one who made
   Jack die."
While someone from the back yelled, "No, 'twas me who laid
   the bully low"
and all the raging hectic while, the woman never lost her smile.

Bill's clientele was brought en bloc to stand indicted in the dock.
The judge said, "It's beyond my ken. How can I hang so many men?"
The lawyer not one story broke as each man claimed he made
        Jack croak.

The judge addressed the tragic lass, through learned hands his words
        were passed
by mental braille which she knew well. The judge's voice rang
        like a bell.
"With sympathy to you Miss Black, I'm sure you know who did attack
the man you planned to wed quite soon, they tell me 'twas to be
        that noon.
Could you point out among this faction, the man who did this deadly
        action?"
Excitement in the courthouse piled, but sweet Flo only sat
        and smiled.

The judge could only end the case. He said, with pity on his face,
"It's plain your heart's been torn apart, for life has been
        no apple-cart.
He killed your dad, and done his time, now someone's added
        to the crime,
and killed the man you planned to wed. The only men you loved
        are dead.
You saddened girl, my heart goes out and to the villain I will shout—
he must be here among this crowd—'Listen slayer, I hope
        you're proud!
This girl was wronged by the man who died, and wronged by
        everyone who lied.
She can't respond because of shock. Someday she may and then
        I'll lock
the cur away until he hangs, or else goes mad with remorse pangs.'"
His teeth were clenched as he angrily hissed, "Ad Nauseam ...
        Case dismissed!"

And sweet Flo wandered in the park and saw (but never heard)
        the lark.
She wandered smiling every day, until her golden hair turned grey.
They found her dead from heart-attack, and scrawled in sand,
        'I loved you Jack.'

45 EARL STREET

I took a walk down Earl Street, maimed and blinded Earl Street.
I took a walk down Earl Street and cried, just like a child.
The street was foul and sated, the houses corrugated,
blinded, gagged, deflated, amid the rubble piled.
Some were gashed already, and stood alone, unsteady.
Somehow proud and ready, yet frightened all the while.

I found the house that reared me. Appearance-wise it scared me.
I spoke. I'm sure it heard me as I walked its saddened hall.
It creaked a muted greeting like gurgled water leaking.
I thought I heard it speaking, saying welcome, welcome home.
I saw the room I'd slept in and very often wept in
when love was unrequited and days were sad and long.

The staircase bore me gladly, my heart was beating madly.
I viewed the bedroom sadly where my parents used to sleep.
Sunlight had streamed around it, before the wreckers found it
and manacled and bound it with concrete blocks and brick.

As I stood there time went flying and I heard my mother crying—
in the parlour saw dad lying in a coffin brown and gold.
I turned quite resolutely, the house observed me mutely,
I studied it astutely and I'm sure I saw it smile.
So walked out into Earl Street, maimed and blinded Earl Street.
I stood awhile in Earl Street and cried, just like a child.

CASUAL CONVERSATION

"What are ye havin' Bob? Bottle an' a half-in? What are ye at the day?
Heysham, Mersey, Bristol, Clyde? God, yer at the spuds ye say.
How'd ye finish up at that Bob ... Ack, ye say, ye came in late.
Ach it's better late than niver, an' sure a man cud have a worser fate
Than trundle bloody spuds all day without a chance to get away
or even git yer breath back.

***

"Here's yer drink now ... sup it up. I was at the Parcel boat.
Finished now, free man again, insurance cards are in me coat.

Wonder what there'll be tomorrow, someone said the flour
   boat's due.
Ach, we'll have to wait an' see, Bob, nothin' else that we can do.

***

"In the mornin', stannin' waitin', then the mad rush through
   the gate,
All the young 'uns, pushin', shovin' ... that's the bit I really hate.
Thanks a lot, I'll have a bottle ... Aye, I'll have a wee one too.
'Member when yis slung the 'rosies'? Where's the big guy worked
   with you?
Strong as an ox he was, thon fella. Good for a laugh, an' always
   funny.
God ... I'm shocked to hear that Bob. Ya say he's buried
   in Carmoney.
Man, I'm really sad to hear that. Hi mate ... givus another drink.
God that guy was in his prime, an' now he's dead. It makes you think.
Used to watch 'im in the houl he niver worried 'bout a thing.
The heaves he slung were straight an' level. Stacked like soldiers
   in the sling.

***

"Thirty-eight ye say he was. Five wee kids he left behind.
It's sad to hear the big lad's buried. Men like him are hard to find.
Heart ye say ... Cuda bin naught else, for sure that big guy worked
   like hell.
Used to watch him ... strong, efficient, when yis slung the Oyster
   Shell.

***

"Feel it now meself sometimes. Dammit Bob, we're gittin' oul.
That work's hard enough for young-uns, toilin' in the blasted coul.
All them years of gettin' soaked ... Shirts turned black with rain
   an' sweat.
We shud be home by the fire. All these years an' no sense yet.

***

"Ack, I wish I'd saved a few bob. So do you ... we're both oul fools.
Only time we'll git some rest is when we win the bloody pools.
Aw c'mon we'll have another. Sentiment's a thing I hate ...
Two more halfs an' two more bottles ... Bob, I'm sorry 'bout
   yer mate."

SUCKERED

I was stannin' in Barney's, just havin' a beer
an' thinkin' the thoughts of the poor.
After boozin' all night, I just didn't feel right.
I was glad I'd enough for a cure.
That's when the bar-room door opened
an' somebody shouted "Repent!
If you don't seek salvation this good day
to the bowels of Hell you'll be sent."

His voice pierced its way through my ear-drums
an' kicked at the pain in my head.
If my poor shattered brain had bin clearer,
I'd have finished the likker an' fled.
His gimlet eye fixed on my features,
his grimy hand clutched at my coat.
"A rich man will not enter Heaven—
them's the truest words ever bin spoke."

He roared this out as he grasped me
an' glared at the drink in my han'.
"The money that bought that," he uttered,
"cuda bought food for some dyin' man."
Now normally I'm not a sucker,
for guys with the gift of the gab,
but this guy had nettled my conscience,
with his wild an' yet accurate stab.

The rain drizzled off the bar-windows
the sky seemed so dull an' so dark.
If I give him my dough, then I'd just have to go
an' wander alone in the park.
But somehow this thought didn't hurt me
as much as the look in his eye.
So I fished my few bob from my pocket
an' reached it to him with a sigh.

He vanished within a few seconds,
I wearily finished my drink,
an' walked through the snug to the bar-door ...
An' what I saw there made me blink!
My religious friend set quite contented

a whiskey an' pint at his side.
"What's this?" I managed to utter ...
"Can't go out. I'd be drenched," he replied.

FIGHTIN' TALK

I could left-hook you over the table,
but that wouldn't prove any point.
I could slay you, like Cain did with Abel,
but that would just break up the joint.
So I'll give you ten seconds to leave her,
and hope that you'll take my advice,
'cause I'm kinda liberal with talking,
but I don't boil my cabbages twice.

You're young and you're tough and you're stubborn.
You want me because I'm the best.
You've beaten the others who faced you.
You think I'll fall just like the rest.
Well, maybe you're right. I've grown older,
my breathing is not what it was
but I'll beat rings round any of you punks,
'cause I fight with my brains, not my jaws.

So if you remain here to face me,
I'll show you how veterans fight.
I'll gouge out your eyes and I'll boot you.
I'll knee you and butt you and bite!
I'll break both your arms and I'll choke you.
I'll bite the ears clean off your head.
I'll kick in your teeth, pull your hair out.
You'll wake in a hospital bed.

So take youself off by the hand boy,
you've got some more inches to grow
before you can mix it with me son ...
and don't slam the door as you go!

LITTLE HELPER

Little helper, leave your shelter, jump into my searching hand,
Firmly nestle 'tween my fingers, snug your stock fits in my palm.
Let your one tooth seek the sackcloth, bury deep; I'll twist
    your head.
You give added strength to my arm (from the wound no products
    bled).

Like a biting nimble puppy, worry each sack to my reach.
Nipping, tipping, never ripping, just a tiny hole in each.
Draw those bags to the elevator, little finger made of steel.
Draw those sacks with prolonged fury (you won't hurt
    the yellow meal).

Just what would I do without you, flesh and bone cringe
    at the thought.
Fingers would get sore and blistered if yourself I hadn't brought.
When the last bag has been lifted and we're brushing up the dirt,
I make sure you nest securely, in the pocket of my shirt.

AN ENLIGHTENED FRIGHTENED FIGHTIN' MAN

I fight with my fists and my boots and my head.
I fight 'cause I don't like to run.
I've belted with zest 'cause I'm poor and oppressed ...
But I don't want to fight with a gun!

A kick in the thigh or a punch in the eye
is nothing compared to the feel
of a bayonet tearing its way through your ribs,
or a lung that's been punctured by steel.

A personal hate fired by rage can create
a reason for combat to start.
And the fire in your eyes for a face you despise,
lights a fuse that's attached to your heart.

Then your fists start to fly as you pummel the guy
with a venom that you really mean ...

But how can you boot at, never mind shoot at,
a fellow that you've never seen.

I'll say it again. I know fighting's insane,
and not to be treated as fun,
but I'll still take a chance with a jab and a dance.
I ain't gonna fight with a gun.

YORK STREET

I just got off the Heysham boat, I landed with a frown.
I looked around the place I loved, the place called Sailorstown.
I was very disappointed when nobody hove in view
and I began to wonder if the song they sang was true.

> *Chorus:* No matter where ye roam my lad,
> no matter where ye flit
> In India, Timbuctoo, Russia or Tibet.
> America, Australia, China or Japan.
> No matter where ye roam my lad,
> You'll find a York Street man.

Just then a fella came in view, he looked me in the face.
Says he, "You're Billy Murphy's son—I'd know ye any place.
I'm glad to see ya home again an' lukin' in the pink,
Come over to the Lifeboat an' we'll have a little drink."

> *Chorus:* No matter where ye roam my lad,
> no matter where ye flit
> In India, Timbuctoo, Russia or Tibet.
> America, Australia, China or Japan.
> No matter where ye roam my lad,
> You'll find a York Street man.

Says he, "I'm thinkin' 'bout the time way back in forty-two.
In France the bombs were fallin' fast, as thick as Irish stew.
We charged with bayonets flailin' an' cut the Gerries down
'cause half of our platoon was born an' reared in Sailorstown."

> *Chorus:* No matter where ye roam my lad,
> no matter where ye flit

In India, Timbuctoo, Russia or Tibet.
America, Australia, China or Japan.
No matter where ye roam my lad,
You'll find a York Street man.

They say when Edmund Hillary conquered Everest,
he sat down rather heavily, his strength sapped by the test.
The abominable snowman around an ice-ridge ran
retreating from a fist-fight with a burly York Street man.

Chorus: No matter where ye roam my lad,
no matter where ye flit
In India, Timbuctoo, Russia or Tibet.
America, Australia, China or Japan.
No matter where ye roam my lad,
You'll find a York Street man.

Now Churchill in his memoirs, he mused an awful lot
about a place in Belfast. It's a tidy little spot.
He said, "If someone peeves you and for war you've got a yen,
never try to win it without some York Street men."

Chorus: No matter where ye roam my lad,
no matter where ye flit
In India, Timbuctoo, Russia or Tibet.
America, Australia, China or Japan.
No matter where ye roam my lad,
You'll find a York Street man.

The Devil he came up from hell and had a look around,
looking for some tough guys to take back underground.
He got them from the Shankill, the Falls and Sandy Row,
but down along old York Street, he was afraid to go.

Chorus: No matter where ye roam me lad,
no matter where ye flit.
In India, Timbuctoo, Russia or Tibet.
America Australia, China or Japan.
No matter where ye roam my lad,
you'll find a York Street man.

SAILORSTOWN

In Sailorstown was some good men and many a punch-up
   we had then,
but we'd all finish friends again, in Sailorstown.
In Sailorstown the drink was good and many men used it for food.
It put them in the fightin' mood, in Sailorstown.
In Sailorstown no copper's nark dared to walk if it was dark.
They didn't cotton to that lark, in Sailorstown.
In Sailorstown the streets were small, not much space wall to wall
Each room no bigger than a horse's stall, in Sailorstown.
In Sailorstown each little street boasted women clean and neat,
the kitchen houses looked a treat, in Sailorstown.
In Sailorstown nobody moaned, although the streets
   were cobblestoned.
Friendship, that was all we owned, in Sailorstown.
In Sailorstown they waked their dead and smiled when two young
   ones were wed.
At births they wet the baby's head, in Sailorstown.
In Sailorstown a motorway sprawls where once tough men held sway,
where happy children used to play, in Sailorstown.
In Sailorstown was some good men, I wish I was back there again.
No finer souls I've met since then, in Sailorstown.

SKINT AGAIN

Skint again! No lesson learned. Fingers ache from being burned.
Good advice? It's all bin spurned, 'cause I'll be back again tomorrow.
Work real hard to get a stake, sling cement without a break,
seems it's all for the bookie's sake 'cause I get left with only sorrow.

Wife gits mad; it's not her fault. I'm just too stubborn to call a halt.
Defeat is sour! It tastes of salt. Aw well, there's a spell to borrow.
Broke again! It's a bitter pill. Seems I'll niver ring the till.
Somehow I know I niver will, but that don't stop me tryin'.

Losers ... Losers ... Makes you sick! Wonder why your head's so thick.
Crawl away, your wounds to lick. You'll try again tomorrow.
Wife needs money! Food is dear. Rent needs payin', kids need gear.
You'll bring it home, she needn't fear, until you reach the bookies.

Git too old to sling cement. Health an' money's all bin spent
chasin' horses the divil sent. Aw well! Roll on the pension!

HELL IS THE HOUL OF A BEG BOAT

Hell is the houl of a beg boat slingin' out forty an hour
after a night on the likker when yer head an' yer belly's on fire.
Yer dodgin' the heaves that go flyin', whipped from the hatch
    to the shore.
Sweat's sweepin' down through yer eyebrows, you slip more than
    once to the floor.
Yer eye's on the hook as it travels, you don't want another sore head.
Yer hands grip the hard paper sackin', yer wishin' yid stayed
    in yer bed.
Yeah! Hell is the houl of a beg boat slingin' out forty an hour
after a night on the likker when yer head an' yer belly's on fire.

You look at yer mate as he labours, he's treatin' it all as a game.
All of his life he's teetotal. Yer wishin' that you were the same.
The ganger is yellin' down at you, the winch-block is screechin'
    for oil,
The shoremen are lappin' ropes round you, yer head feels
    like it's on the boil.
Yeah! Hell is the houl of a beg boat slingin' out forty an hour
after a night on the likker when yer head an' yer belly's on fire.

The winch hook comes swingin' in at you. You grab it an' hook
    on yer heave.
The salt in yer sweat burns yer eyeballs, you wipe it away
    with yer sleeve.
You shout for a bucket of water, the ganger looks down with a leer,
"I'll run down to Barney's," he chortles, "an' git you a nice pint
    of beer."
Yeah! Hell is the houl of a beg boat slingin' out forty an hour
after a night on the likker when yer head an' yer belly's on fire.

Yer mate spreads the sling an' the canvas an' tells you it's your turn
    to sink,
You claw at the sacks with yer fingers, yid sell yer left leg for a drink.
The trick is to dig out the cargo with nothin' except yer bare hands.

You toss the first beg down behind you an' choke in the dust
    as it lands.
Yeah! Hell is the houl of a beg boat slingin' out forty an hour ,
After a night on the likker when yer head an' yer belly's on fire.

Yer burrowin' just like a rabbit, tail over head in a bin.
You snarl for a bucket of water, the ganger just gives you a grin.
The sweepin' hook won't let you linger, you've got to keep sendin'
    out heaves.
You hook on then start to another. You can't even watch as it leaves.
The paper-sacks burnin' yer fingers as down through the cargo
    you bore.
Yer tossin' up begs to yer buddy an' prayin' yill soon see the floor.
Yeah! Hell is the houl of a beg boat slingin' out forty an hour
after a night on the likker when yer head an' yer belly's on fire.

Yer haulin' an' draggin' an' stackin' until you at last see the floor.
Yer buddy drops in there beside you an' soon you make room
    for two more.
From then on the rest is plain sailin', you clear out the wings
    an' the nose.
When the last ton is winched to the shore gang, you heave
    a deep sigh as it goes.
Yeah! Hell is the houl of a beg boat spewin' out forty an hour
after a night on the likker ... when yer head an' yer belly's on fire.

THE TUG-BOAT SAILOR

I was stannin' at the corner, when up came little Jim.
Says he, "I'm lukin' for our kid, I've got a job for him".
But Bouncer didn't want it. That's how I came to be
An O.S. on a tug-boat, the day I went to sea.
We made for Barney Vallely's, as all good seamen did
And lowered stout an' Bannerman (Jim subbed me half-a-quid).
Says he, "It's time we motored, we're sailin' with the tide."
I hurried through the dockgates filled with Bannermans an' pride.

We headed for the basin, where all the tug-boats lay.
Arriving there quite breathless, we watched her sail away.
Says Jim, "We'll catch her next time," as we watched the seagulls
    swarm.

"C'mon; a spot of shore leave won't do you any harm."
We headed back to Barney's an' drank Bannermans an' stout.
In truth, I didn't worry if the boat was in or out.
But Jim was made of sterner stuff. His life revolved in salt.
We staggered into Whitla Street an' made the traffic halt.

Our ship was in the basin, tied by head an' heel.
The skipper eyed us from the bridge an' watched us rock an' reel.
Dressed like a civilian, a cloth cap adorned his head.
He looked at my limp figure, an' ordered me to bed.
When I woke the ship was tossin'. I felt sicker than a dog
for that night had all the mixtures of storm an' rain an' fog.
Wee Jim came down the ladder, his voice was warm an' bright—
"I'm glad to see yer shipshape, for we've work to do tonight."

He helped me up the ladder, onto the open deck, the ship lurched
In the weather. I had a sick attack!
I grimly hugged the boat's rail as my cargo spluttered out
An' filled the scuppers ankle-deep in Bannerman's an' stout.
But wee Jim says, "C'mon now, there's work we gotta do
For this ship is a dry ship, except for me an' you.
An' though we love our likker, we've gotta make it plain
That we can do our duty, be it snow or hail or rain."

I did my duty that night, although the squall howled high.
I stood my tug-boat station, an' heeded every cry.
Though froze from bone to marrow, an' drenched from head to toe
I wouldn't leave my station until Jimmy bade me go.
Well anyway from that day I never missed a tide,
I did my turn efficiently with Jimmy at my side.
We worked hard on the high tide, but whenever it went out,
We sauntered down to Barney's an' drank Bannerman's an' stout.

TALE OF A SPUD BOAT

Monty an' Devil an' Smoke were ashore,
Closey an' Lyttle an' two or three more.
J.O. had the book with his back to the door,
the day we loaded the Caroline.
Winkie an' Wilsey an' Joe in the houl,

Gibby was drivin' the winch with a scowl,
Scadger was puffin' because of the coul.
The day we loaded the Caroline.

The sailor said, "We're for two hundred ton,
so up to the cobblers I'll be able to run.
'Cause it's gonna be late when youse are done.
The day we loaded the Caroline
Nicolson showed us the spuds we'd to lift,
an' so we proceeded the pile for to shift.
The winch was fast an' the boat was a gift.
The day we loaded the Caroline.

Majestics, King Edwards an' Consuls all were
stowed in the hatch with the greatest of care.
You load up the truck an' you run like a hare.
The day we loaded the Caroline.
By noon the ship was ready for sea,
an' gently movin' away from the quay.
A job well done, with that you'll agree.
The day we loaded the Caroline.

The sailor came runnin' outa the shed,
an' managed to leap on the fo'c'sle head.
He shook his fist an' his face was red.
The day we loaded the Caroline.
He scowled at us as he sailed past
an' snarled, "No men cud work that fast."
For his boots were still on the cobbler's last.
The day we loaded the Caroline.

He said next time that he'd take note,
not to try an' leave the boat,
In fact he wudn't put on his coat,
when next we load the Caroline.

SONG OF A SHIP

When the fog lies low on the harbour, and the quays are bare
    and bleak
It's then I find on the waterfront the solitude I seek.
The giant, sleek ocean-going ladies overshadow me as I walk.
Oh, what tales they would tell of distant lands if only they could talk.

Some have been stripped of their cargoes and lie with their bowels
    bare.
Others are deep in the water, carrying more than their share.
Footsteps ring as an alien walks some deserted deck.
Perhaps he's dreaming of his own shores and wishing he was back.

It's early and the sleeping ships are beautiful in repose.
Somewhere beyond my vision, a mournful fog-horn blows.
Those restless ships don't like it, being tied by head and heel.
They'd rather race unbridled, with the master at the wheel.
With screeching growls she'll weigh the rusty anchor to her side
And roll to sea from the shabby quay, on the breast of the morning
    tide.

BELFAST DOCKS

When I was young, I took the road that those who came before me
    strode.
I stood with the crowds in the cobbled pen where the gangers
    schooled the casual men
The work was tough, the conditions bad, and it didn't help to be
    a lad,
for the ganger's eyes would pierce and scan as he probed the school
    for an all-round man
who could sling and stow or drive a winch. Which skills like these
    you'd be a cinch
to work each day in the ship or shed, but now it seems
    those times have fled.
Forklift truck and container box ... you've torn the life from Belfast
    Dock ...

Used to be you'd have toiled two weeks in a timber boat, using long
    sharp cleeks,

Working night and day till the holds were clear, sweating under
    the ganger's sneer.
Whilst splinters tear your hands to pieces, the jibing foreman never
    ceases
As he goads you on to perfect his plan to mould another all-round
    man.
One he can use or discard at whim, for you're just a face in the
    crowd to him.
But your painful learning when you were young has come to naught
    now the wood's preslung.
Pelletised timber in four-ton block ... you've torn the life from Belfast
    Dock.

Livestock travel in mobile pens from Irish farms to Scottish glens,
They reach their destinations quick, without a tap from a docker's
    stick,
And yet it isn't so long ago when dockers travelled to and fro.
I still can hear the baleful bleats of beasts being herded
    through narrow streets,
Where we as kids would help bring back, those which ran off
    from the pack.
Frightened creatures, from a steaming herd in Princess Dock Street,
    running scared.
Mobile cranes and crated livestock ... you've torn the life from
    Belfast Dock.

Now I muse as I watch the scenes of ships unloaded by huge
    machines,
Stripping hatches in record time. Sometimes progress can be
    a crime.
More work done by fewer men, most are left in the schooling pen.
Mechanical shovels scooping bulk. It's enough to make a bagman
    sulk
for bag-boats used to be ten-a-penny, now you'll find there's hardly
    any
as these giant monsters clear the quay, quick as you'd drink a cup
    of tea.
Dieselled horses working 'round the clock, you've torn the life from
    Belfast Dock.

Empty berths and cranes a'wasting. Flattened sheds and tarmacked
    basin,
Forktruck ... Shovel ... Bulk and Block ... you've torn the life from
    Belfast Dock.

SUCKERED AGAIN

"If I'd bin thirty when he was thirty, I'd have tried him an' not felt
    so dirty,
but now he's kinda lost his sting, an' to beat him now wudn't mean
    a thing."
So said Dandy McIntyre, sittin' at the pub's big fire,
drinkin' pints 'cause they were free, bought by mugs like you an' me
who always like to hear the crack when fightin' men their fights
re-act.

"Once I felled Big Jimmy Jones. I nearly busted all his bones
    with one great blow,
which I swear to all, had I missed, wuda carried me through
    the wall."
"We all know it's not strength you lack," a little voice piped
    from the back,
"An' though your talk's all guts an' fire, you don't fool me,
    Big McIntyre.
You cudn't beat Big Jim McKee, if you were thirty, an' he was three."

Dandy's face got very red. "Lissen, squirt, it's like I said,
McKee's past thirty an' lost his sting, an' to bate him now wudn't
    mean a thing."
"Ack, talk is chape," said the little man, "but now I'm gonna force
    your han' ...
A fiver each, Mac, that's the call. Big Jim an' you, an' winner
    takes all."
"Man that sounds great, I'd love to fight, but sure, I haven't
    got a light."

"Now Mac a fightin' man like you should have his backers,
    like we do,
an' if you can't back-up your talk, then you know you shouldn't
    squalk."
Dandy face was rather grey, as the pip-squeak turned an' walked
    away.
Just then I had a winning notion. "Hold it! I'll put forth a motion,
among us here, we'll raise the dough, if to the fight you'll let us go."

Both men gave us their consent an' so we gathered up the rent,
an' went to watch 'em in a field, to see who'd be the first to yield.
Dandy McIntyre looked great, Jim McKee seemed underweight.
When the bettin' had begun, Jim McKee was three to one.

We shovelled dough on McIntyre, because he showed the pep
an' fire.

The little squirt took every bet, said our notes wud all be met.
Anyway they squared aroun', then McIntyre was on the groun'
grovellin' from a mighty punch an' clutchin' where he put his lunch.
When he didn't rise again, I saw our dough go down the drain.
Jim McKee had scooped the pool! Man, I felt an awful fool.

Now I know how that sayin' started, about a fool an' his money
soon bein' parted,
'cause I'm sure the punch that felled the hard, missed him
by a half-a-yard.
An' it didn't seem to do much harm, cos them three walked off
arm-an'-arm
an' while we're left with only pence, they're drinkin' Scotch
at our expense.

THE MAN INSIDE

The man inside set me aside. His hard cold eyes gleamed at his prey.
My body moved to his every whim. I didn't want to get in his way.
This was not me, this tough-faced gent. His every move gained
new respect.
He eyed his foe. His voice was low. He said, "You move an' you'll
be decked."

The foe was brave. His face to save, he moved and tried to throw
a punch.
My body swayed. My two feet stayed. His rib-cage cracked beneath
the crunch.
I shifted feet, he smelt defeat and tried, in vain, to move inside.
He threw a right with all his might. This blow I deftly tossed aside.

And then I threw the punch I knew would smash on his bewildered
face.
He hit the deck and I stood back, to give the guy some breathin'
space.
When he let it show he didn't want to know, the man inside
slowed down.
He wins each fight I get him in: the man inside don't give
no ground.

JAB AND MOVE

dedicated to every man who boxed for a living.
(And a 'big hand' for the losers.)

Jab and move it. Jab and move it. There is something you must
   prove.
Jab and move it, you must prove it. Throw that left out. Jab
   and move.
He's a fighter and you're lighter. He's as hard as obo nails.
So don't chance it. Jab and dance it. Float it whilst his strength
   prevails.

He's a heavy and the levy of his punch could knock you down.
Jab and wing him. Float and sting him. Keep your cool or else
   you'll drown,
drown beneath a storm of punches that will rock you to your core.
His body feels it as you weal it. Raw and red and splotched and sore.

So jab and move it you can prove it—brain can often master might.
You can prove it, jab and cruise it. Left, left, left, hold high
   your right.
See his face-flesh split and curdle, see his eyes turn black with blood.
Keep your right up and the spite up. Nip his counters in the bud.

Now his mouth is wide and gaping. Jab and move it, there's
   the proof.
Brain can often beat the brawler, make that left sing,
   Bouf Bouf Bouf.
Now his eyes are blank, unseeing. Cross your right hand,
   fast and slick.
Watch him topple like an apple, reach that neutral corner quick.

Hear the ref count out the seconds, see him strive to gain his feet.
Leap in triumph. He won't make it and he grovels in defeat.
Now the ref will raise your gloved hand, as again you grin and leap,
leap one more rung up the ladder. Boy, you jab and move so sweet.

WHAT DOES IT MATTER?

What does it matter what puts you out?
The bomb or the gun or the legalised shout,
The UVF or the IRA; the men who burn, or the men who pray?
The Hibernian Lodge or the Orange band,
the bailiff or the Lords of the Land?
The racketeer, or the hate-filled note,
that the neighbour inflamed with insanity wrote?
The sinister men with their feathers and tar,
The merchants of death in their weapon-filled car?
The fellow who draws at the map of the town
red-lining the houses he wants to knock down,
who couldn't care less if you end in a ditch,
so long as his new ring-road runs without hitch?
The gifted orators who fashion the hate that spews
from the fitter or plumber or mate
who fan it with porter and then heave a stone
at the home of some old one who lives all alone?
What does it matter what puts you out,
be it progress, injustice, or small-minded lout?
Or the midnight marauder whose bigoted shriek,
sends terror to bed with the aged and weak?
What does it matter what puts you out,
when you're old and alone and just can't get about?
And you're plucked from your roots like an unwanted weed ...
What does it matter whose hand did the deed?

MY DADDY FOUGHT FOR IRELAND

My daddy fought for Ireland and died to make it free.
My daddy thought for Ireland, I wish he'd thought for me.
I'm just a little fellow and I miss him hugging me.
My daddy died for Ireland. I wish he'd lived for me.

My daddy loved his Ulster, and fought to keep it free.
My daddy bled for Ulster, I wish he'd stayed for me.
I'm just a little fellow and miss climbing on his knee.
My daddy died for Ulster. I wish he'd lived for me.

My daddy lived to keep the peace and died that it could be.
My daddy tried to reason, that all men should be free.
But though I'm proud of daddy, there's no arms to cradle me.
My daddy died for freedom. I wished he'd lived for me.

THE SPORTSMAN'S ARMS

Just opposite Brougham Street, it sits in a nook,
where York Street lies sprawled like an unfinished book.
The years have swam by it, but now it's no more.
The thread has bin spun. Barney's closin' the door.

He sold damn good likker to Jim, Jack or Joe.
It was commonly known that he hadn't a foe.
He also sold heaven to heads that were sore.
But the deed has bin done. Barney's closin' the door.

We had some good times in that beat-up old boozer.
He'd give you some heart if you backed the last loser,
then slip you a stake to get goin' once more.
But that's all behind us. He's closin' the door.

The guys whom he's leavin' are soon gonna know
we won't meet his equal wherever we go.
Professional, down to his soft-hearted core,
an era has ended. He's closin' the door.

A JUG OF BARNEY'S WINE.

The fight was goin' bad for Jim, he'd hit the canvas twice
an' Kelly's left was cuttin' him as if it were a knife,
but Big Jim turned the tables with a punch that was divine,
when his second soaked his gumshield in a jug of Barney's wine.

It could fly aeroplanes or fuel trains
or 'juice' a shipside crane.
It banished ills, done away with pills,
and made redundant pain.

Wee Tammy couldn't get a girl because he was quite small.
He'd chat 'em up quite bravely, but they'd never never fall.
But now he knocks 'em sideways, lookin' down from six-foot nine,
since his mama washed his stockings in a jug of Barney's wine.

It could fly aeroplanes or fuel trains
or 'juice' a shipside crane.
It banished ills, done away with pills,
and made redundant pain.

Bob Johnston had a stammer, it made his life a hell.
When he began a story, it would take a year to tell.
But now at Queens he lectures, in a voice that's sure and fine,
since his granny soaked his dentures in a jug of Barney's wine.

It could fly aeroplanes or fuel trains
or 'juice' a shipside crane.
It banished ills, done away with pills,
an' made redundant pain.

It clears the grit from binmen's throats, it helps the dockers
    empty boats,
it makes the sailors feel quite gay, and sends the carters on
    their way ...
And underneath each coat you'll find, the magic known
    as Barney's wine.

FREEDOM FIGHTER

What do you see when you dream, freedom fighter,
what do you see when you dream?
Do the corpses walk? Do the mutilated scream?
What do you see when you dream?

What do you see in the gloom, freedom fighter,
what do you see in the gloom?
Do the spectres lurk in the corner of your room?
What do you see in the gloom?

What do you think when you sing, freedom fighter,
what do you think when you sing?

Do you think what you did was a glorious thing?
What do you think when you sing?

What will you do when you die, freedom fighter
What will you do when you die?
When they take your gun and there's nowhere to run ...
What will you do when you die?

YORK STREET FLUTE

> *Chorus:* There's niver bin a band like York Street Flute,
> be it brass band or silver, cavalry or foot.
> From Rangoon to Rathcoole, from Russia to Kilroot,
> there's niver bin a band like York Street Flute.

They blow up the Shankill, they blow up Sandy Row,
they'd blow up the Falls, but the cops won't let 'em go.
They'll blow 'til they're purple, steppin' out in style.
If you wash 'em down with whiskey, man, they'll walk a million mile.

> *Chorus:* There's niver bin a band like York Street Flute,
> be it brass band or silver, cavalry or foot.
> From Rangoon to Rathcoole, from Russia to Kilroot,
> there's niver bin a band like York Street Flute.

Dempsey played the lead drum; a man of high renown.
He's known in every village, every hamlet, every town.
Some say he's sixty, others say he ain't ...
But we're all aware his favourite word is Pint, Pint, Pint.

> *Chorus:* There's niver bin a band like York Street Flute,
> be it brass band or silver, cavalry or foot.
> From Rangoon to Rathcoole, from Russia to Kilroot,
> there's niver bin a band like York Street Flute.

They walked with the Seaver Lodge, one mornin' in July,
They went to the Master's house an' drank the poor man dry.
But when they strode along the road, their play was smooth as silk,
although they'd drunk most everything, except the baby's milk.

Chorus: There's niver bin a band like York Street Flute,
be it brass band or silver, cavalry or foot.
From Rangoon to Rathcoole, from Russia to Kilroot,
there's niver bin a band like York Street Flute.

The last time I saw 'em, they walked into Lewis Street.
Blew out an' spewed out, they cud hardly stan' their feet.
The cops who were with them, tried to lend a han',
by becomin' dummy-fluters, for the York Street band.

Chorus: There's niver bin a band like York Street Flute,
be it brass band or silver, cavalry or foot.
From Rangoon to Rathcoole, from Russia to Kilroot,
there's niver bin a band like York Street Flute.

Whenever there was trouble, they always got the blame.
They changed their name a hundred times,
but still remained the same.
Dempsey's gone, but they still plod on
each year they walk the route,
but no matter what they call themselves,
they're still the York Street Flute.

There's niver bin a band like York Street Flute,
be it brass band or silver, cavalry or foot.
From Rangoon to Rathcoole, from Russia to Kilroot.
There's niver bin a band like York Street Flute.

BELFAST 69-76

Belfast is a sullen town, spawned upon a stream,
born to cries of murder, and midwifed by a scream.
Belfast is a bleak town with dull and dark mean streets
where man greets with suspicion every stranger that he meets.

Belfast is a sad town, its moods are deep and black,
sometimes it fights to shake the mites of hatred from its back.
Belfast has been martyred by men who hold it dear
and Belfast has been bartered by men who hide a sneer.

Belfast has been pummelled by men who find it fun
to beat it into debris by bomb, grenade and gun.
Belfast is a sullen town, spawned upon a stream,
born to cries of murder, and midwifed by a scream.

SATURDAY NIGHT IN YORK STREET

The smell of pig's feet boilin', with ribs an' nabs an' noints,
greeted all the menfolk as they rolled home from the joints.
Mother cut the soup-greens whilst waitin' for her sire,
then bathed the children briskly in a tub beside the fire.
That was Saturday night in York Street, boyhood memories remain.
Saturday night in York Street will never come again.

When dad rolled up the hall half-drunk, you'd ask him for a wing.
Of course you wouldn't get it until he'd heard you sing.
He'd sit among his cronies and make 'em all keep hush,
as you stood there, knees a tremblin' and warbled like a thrush.
That was Saturday night in York Street, pappa liked an old refrain.
Saturday night in York Street will never come again.

You'd get to pour some Guinness and help hand round the soup,
whilst songs were sang impromptu, by the happy, friendly group.
Your mum and dad would giggle as you hid behind the sink,
pretending not to notice when you stole a little drink.
That was Saturday night in York Street, empty bottles you
      would drain.
Saturday night in York Street will never come again.

Being carried up to bed by a rather shaky dad,
who tucked you in with tenderness, for he loved his little lad.
He'd leave the mantle flickering 'cause he knew you liked to hear
the melodies that drifted from the voices sweet and clear.
Saturday night in York Street brings a tear I can't contain.
Saturday night in York Street will never come again.

SING A SONG OF YORK STREET

Sing a song of York Street, take me back again,
to Big Davy and Buck Alec as they brawl in Stable Lane.
With doffers screamin' round 'em, they fought a brutal bout.
Wearin' only trousers with their bellies hangin' out.
Tell me 'bout the chancers, the hard-chaws an' the brass.
Sing a song about the days that all too soon have passed.
The square-setts an' the paviors an' the gas-lamps have all gone.
The characters have vanished, but the memories linger on.
Tell me 'bout the pawnshops where yis went when times were bleak,
an' pawned the oul lad's Sunday suit to see yis through the week.
Tell me more of Rinty and how he won his crown.
On that night yis lit a Bony' that was seen all over town.
Heagan's home-baked sodas, Wilson's boiled pig's feet.
Barney Conway's Guinness, Fenton's finest meat.
Buttermilk from Turners. Geordie's fresh ice-cream.
The Queens and Joe McKibbens; all have vanished like a dream.
Sometimes I wander down there an' sorta make the rounds.
I see them in my mind's eye, an' hear their phantom sounds.
I hear their tumblers clinkin' an' see their faces plain.
Please sing a song of York Street an' take me back again.

from
AN OUL JOBBIN' POET
(1989)

AN OUL JOBBIN' POET

I'm an oul jobbin' poet, born outa my time,
if you buy me a likker, I'll read you a rhyme.
I'm not hard to pay, a wee lager and lime ...
If yer flyin', I'll take a quick half-in.

I can render a poem that's fairly well known
or maybe yid like to hear one of me own,
but my throat's kinda raspy and dry as a stone ...
just another wee sip ... Now we're laughin' ...

I know millions of poems, wud you like a wee song?
I've a fine pair of lungs an' a voice that's quite strong.
Just top up me tumbler. It won't take me long.
Pour away. Man, yer hand's fine and steady.

Here's one of me own. It's well written and slick.
An ode guaranteed to bring tears from a brick.
It's all about wimmen who two-time and trick.
Just another wee sip. Then I'm ready.

There's nothin' like wimmin to make a man cringe,
They girn an' they yap if you go on a binge.
When yer sleepin' it off, yer oul ribs get a dinge.
Their ignorance wud drive ye to drinkin'.

Wud ye like to hear 'Cargoes', or maybe 'Drake's Drum'?
Somethin' from Kipling wud make this place hum.
Do you think I cud have a wee coke with this rum?
They tell me it stimulates thinkin'.

I'm an oul jobbin' poet in love with me art,
there's acres of literature locked in me heart.
Just give me a nudge when you want me to start ...
In the meantime, shake a leg with that bottle.

A SONG FOR BARBARA

Sometimes it seems we are losing our way, girl.
Lying like strangers, on long lonely nights.
You read your quota of romantic novels,
Whilst I indulge in long fanciful flights.

Seems like I've grown inattentive and restless,
chasing a dream I may never attain.
Married in theory to paper and pencil,
knowing my thoughtlessness causes you pain.

Often the rainbow I never tire chasing
shines in the light that looks out of your eyes,
making me feel I should ask your forgiveness,
instead of indulging in poetic sighs.

Vague and forgetful and given to silence,
engrossed in a world non-existent to you.
When I'm depressed by a lack of fulfilment,
your smile is a light that is constant and true.

I hope you'll forgive this old scribbling dreamer,
floating on some metaphorical cloud,
striving with all of the power in his being,
composing a lyric to make you feel proud.

THE CLASS OF SIXTY-NINE

Greetings from an old friend, hope this letter finds you well.
I've sad news from this sad land where you once used to dwell.
The tears that stain the pages fall from these eyes of mine.
There's only you and me left from the class of sixty-nine.

The class of sixty-nine, dear old pals for whom I pine—
not one lived to see a dream fulfilled.
Their young fresh faces laugh on this faded photograph.
But today that childish laughter has been stilled.

Andy set a bomb off, when he opened his front door.
Barney took the gas-tube, no one knows what for.

Francie was a peeler, his landrover hit a mine.
There's only you and me left from the class of sixty-nine.

We were bright and cheerful in those days of long ago.
Death lurked on the corner, but how were we to know?
You went to America, we remained behind.
There's only you and me left from the class of sixty-nine.

Willie Bell was knee-capped and died from gangrene.
Gunmen murdered Johnston, for what they thought he'd seen.
Sammy got his head blown off, for stepping out of line.
There's only you and me left, from the class of sixty-nine.

Just one thing left to tell you and it's difficult to write.
I killed two men last summer, in a brutal ghetto fight.
I'm writing from a jail cell, where I'll end this life of mine.
There's only you and me left from the class of sixty-nine.

The class of sixty-nine lie in caskets made of pine.
All are dead and most of them were killed.
Their young fresh faces laugh on this faded photograph.
But today that childish laughter has been stilled.

WAGE NEGOTIATIONS YORK STREET STYLE.
A true story in verse

Davy rose up when we opened the door,
scowlin' because he'd bin roused from his snore.
We numbered three, but I wished we'd bin more,
for Davy was deadly when drowsy.
Alec the Scotsman was stood on my right.
A born entertainer who loved gettin' tight,
he'd the soul of a poet, but he couldn't fight.
His instinct for aggro was lousy.

Hughey the oldest was far from afraid.
His mind was as sharp as a rapier blade
but now he demurred like a virginal maid,
as Davy's eyes picked him for slaughter.

The minute I said, "Can we talk about wages?"
Davy threw one of his terrible rages.
He screamed and he trembled for what seemed like ages
Then knocked Hughey dead with a blatter.

Jock took one look at our friend on the floor,
then ran over home, slammed the bolt on the door.
Davy's ma screamed, "Ack, don't hit them no more,"
an' then started wailin' an' cryin'.
Ignorin' her protests, he grabbed at my throat,
An' snarled, "Ye wee upstart, yev worked yer last boat."
I lost my temper an' threw off my coat.
This action sent oul granny flyin'.

He stopped as she fell like a stone to the floor,
I kept up my guard as I edged to the door.
The wee kitchen shook with his ear-splittin' roar,
so out of that room I went racin'.
If oul granny snuffed it, they'd blame it on me,
an' Davy had brothers who'd kill you for free.
Though they were my uncles, that wouldn't save me—
they'd line up to give me a lacin'.

He ran out behind me, we fought in the street.
From the very beginnin' his strength had me beat.
They stopped it before I was smashed to defeat,
from a cut in my face blood was seepin'.
I fled for my life through the lane to our door.
I prayed Granny English was not hurt or sore,
for the little boy in me had surfaced once more ...
an' much to my shame he was weepin'.

I AM

I am a song that someone is singing.
Strident yet soft, joyous yet sad.
For just as long as the singer is singing,
I must continue through good times and bad.

I am a book that someone is reading,
Turning the pages with each passing day.
Until the last page is turned by the reader,
I am committed to life come what may.

I am a story that someone is writing,
each day a blank page is filled by the prose.
And when the nib has been dipped for the last time,
then I will dwell where a passing thought goes.

SONG OF AN EXILE

Did ya ever walk down York Street when the rain is swirlin' down,
an' the street is so deserted you can see right into town?
Ya can see the Co's big buildin', ya kin see the hawker's stall.
If it wasn't for the rain-clouds, ya cud see the City Hall.

Did ya ever walk down York Street when the snow is peltin' down,
when the young lads grab the doffers an' throw 'em to the ground,
an' belt 'em all with snowballs, or shove snow down their backs ...
When all is white an' covered, except the trammy tracks?

Did ya ever walk down York Street, when the sun is shinin' bright?
If yer down by Gallahers an', if the time is right,
the street is filled with lassies, an' every one a queen,
lukin' so resplendent in their smocks of emerald green.

Did ya ever walk down York Street, headin' for a ship,
an' breathe its air in deeply, an' let a tear-drop slip?
I did the day I left it. Though I've roamed the world I find,
in rain or snow or sunshine, my street is on my mind.

THE MUSE

A muse flew into my idle brain
in an effort to couple a word-filled train,
but thoughts wouldn't muster at Platform One.
It seems there was nowhere they wanted to run.

They wouldn't go forward, they wouldn't go back,
reluctant to travel on memory's track.
I offered to help, in a half-hearted way
and glanced at my pen on the desk where it lay.

Had telekinesis been at my command
the pen would have lifted and flown to my hand.
The muse screamed for action and bellowed with rage,
but thoughts wouldn't stray to that spotless white page.

My pen lay impotent, the page remained blank
as the muse fought in vain with my memory bank.
The maddened muse hollered and begged for some steam
but my mind had succumbed to a fog-coloured dream.

The muse flew away from my bone-idle brain.
Perhaps it will never reside there again.

I'M SINGING JUST FOR YOU

I got an ache inside me when I saw your lovely face,
I'm still haunted by your beauty, and my mind just can't erase
the memories that engulf me as you dance across the floor,
I guess I love you just as much as I loved you once before.

> *Chorus:* And all my pain's out there parading,
> I can't hide it from your eyes
> as you float across the dance floor
> with a string of handsome guys.
> How can I perform my love songs
> and pretend you don't exist,
> when I'm shattered by your nearness
> and the memory of your kiss.

I've been on the road for ages and I've been with countless girls,
as I buried my emotions in a string of endless whirls,
now you've walked into my life again, and even though we're
    through,
I may be looking at the others, but I'm singing just for you.

    Chorus: And all my pain's out there parading,
    I can't hide it from your eyes
    as you float across the dance floor
    with a string of handsome guys.
    How can I perform my love songs
    and pretend you don't exist,
    when I'm shattered by your nearness
    and the memory of your kiss.

THE CURE

For years I'd been plagued with insomnia
    that kept me awake every night.
I'd fought it with Guinness and Horlicks,
    but nothing could put it to flight.

I'd lie from the dusk till the dawning,
    counting as thousands of sheep
gambolled across grassy meadows,
    but nothing could put me to sleep.

One night as I fumed in the darkness,
    I suddenly thought it a crime
to lie in my bed doing nothing,
    so I figured I'd use up the time.

I would fill up a tape with my verses,
    and listen to myself recite.
I'd more than enough poems written
    to carry me through any night.

I could play them each hour I was wakened
    and then when I'd learned them by heart,
I could stand in my local declaiming ...
    and give them a taste of my art.

That night I filled up my recorder
    with verses inspiring and deep.
I heard just about half a stanza
    before I fell into a sleep.

I go out like a light every night now,
    my eyes automatically close.
I'm embarrassed to tell you the potion
    was a dose of my own deathless prose.

Now I'm fresh as a daisy each morning,
    but how can a fellow rejoice,
knowing the factum that floored him,
    was the sound of his verse-reading voice.

THE HARDEST GAME

*A tribute in verse to John McGreevy. Fighting under the name of Jackie
Quinn, he became the Irish featherweight champion in 1929 and the Irish
bantamweight champion in 1935. A native of Belfast's Sailorstown, he was a
credit to the game and a local hero to both sides of the dockland community.*

Born in Sailorstown in Nineteen Ten
he became the doyen of the dockside men,
when he took up boxing and changed his name
to take his chances in the hardest game.

He was Jackie Quinn when the gloves were laced,
and he asked no quarter from the men he faced.
Fistic perfection was his sole aim.
He was dedicated to the hardest game.

This natural flyweight, with style and skill
boxed his way to the top of the bill.
Wild opponents were rendered tame,
as he climbed the ladder in the hardest game.

Young and fearless, fit and trim.
The Warnock brothers all fell to him.
But defeat by Jackie brought little shame
for he was a master of the hardest game.

An Irish champion when just nineteen.
Said Jimmy Warnock, "He's the best I've seen.
Not too many will douse his flame.
He's all our daddies in the hardest game."

The canny fighter with aggressive drive
took the bantamweight title in thirty-five.
And when Mussen punished his courageous frame,
he refused to be halted in the hardest game.

Admired and respected by all since then,
revered by the cream of our fighting men,
whatever religion. they'll say the same—
he gave his all to the hardest game.

When he finally fell it was no disgrace,
for he took on a champion we all must face.
He battled well, but the last count came ...
and we lost a legend of the hardest game.

A WRY OBSERVATION

My Uncle Davy liked things fried in gravy.
Quite fond of tippin' his meat into drippin'
He didn't know lard makes your arteries hard.
His end he did quicken by eating roast chicken.
Whilst still finger-lickin', his ticker stopped tickin'.

How fragile we are! So unlike a car.
It thrives on good greasin' whilst we die a-wheezin'.
But if, as they say, we return in some way,
I think he should plan to come back as a van.

CAGNEY'S NOT DEAD!
Tribute to a legend

Cagney's not dead! How could he be?
He's trapped in the tube for eternity.
Sometimes a G-man, or hood on the lam,
or a doughboy in France fighting for Uncle Sam.

Cagney's not dead! He's still filling the screen,
giving each role an impeccable sheen.
Thrill to his psycho, complete with lips curled,
hollering, "Look Ma! Top of the world."

Cagney's not dead! He's still winning our hearts,
breathing his fire into lack-lustre parts.
Putting an uppity cop in his place,
or shoving a grapefruit in some dumb broad's face.

Cagney's not dead! With a 'wing and a buck',
he portrays an old trouper down on his luck.
Breathtaking dancing, and show-stopping songs
bring that year's Oscar to where it belongs.

Cagney's not dead! Not by a long chalk.
He stalks the last mile in his much copied walk.
Shrugging aside those who'd soothe his despair,
Did Rocky turn yellow when faced with the chair?

Cagney's not dead! He's still strutting his stuff.
Enriching the life of each cinema buff.
Charming, or menacing, hero or lout,
he'll taunt and entrance us till time flickers out.
    Cagney's not dead!

THE ACTOR

I was out with this geezer, a real woman pleaser
with beer in the freezer and whiskey galore.
His outlook was sunny, his patter was funny,
he'd plenty of money and was always half-tore.

His dad's a director, but he's a defector,
an out-of-work actor and running to fat.
He lives for just boozin' and going pub-cruisin',
and loves oozin' Shakespeare and fellas like that.

He'd sit on a bar-stool like he was in play-school
and give us a mouthful of Byron and Shaw.
He'd get kinda racy reciting O'Casey,
with dialogue pacy he held us in awe.

But for all his romancin' and spoutin' and dancin'
I found myself glancing at him in surprise.
Entranced by his acting and image-projecting,
the crowd was neglecting the tears in his eyes.

CHRISTMAS IN YORK STREET 1944

When Tommy and I heard the old staircase creak,
we half-closed our eyes, but continued to peek.
We'd snuggled for hours in our big double bed,
now came the moment for which we'd both prayed.
"That must be Santa," Tom whispered to me,
his face a confusion of terror and glee.
"Doesn't he come down the chimney?" I said,
for mother had cleaned it with lots of black-lead.

Said Tommy the eldest, as loud as he dares;
"He musta come in by the big range downstairs.
I'm sure I heard footsteps, I swear it's the truth,
like someone was tip-toeing over our roof."
A noise on the stair struck us suddenly mute.
I hoped he would find where the stockings were put.
Baggy and roomy, the kind sailors wore,
we'd begged them from Daddy, because they held more.

The bedroom door squeaked and the handle turned slow,
we quietly trembled from temple to toe.
The door opened widely, and there stood our Da!
Being held up by a half-amused Ma.
"That isn't Santa," I thought, filled with dread,

"Maybe he's fell off the roof and he's dead!
That's it,"—I mused, watching through narrowed eyes—
"Daddies must fill in, if Santa Claus dies."

Dad looked as if he himself might be ill,
till Ma hissed, "I think you've drunk more than your fill.
You've always stayed sober on each Christmas Eve."
"Ach, Sarah," he whispered, "I've just started leave ...
I've had a few drinks with my shipmates," he grinned,
and just at that moment, we heard him break wind.
It came like a fog-horn, a long mournful sound ...
and went on for ages until it died down.

From under the blankets spontaneous laughter
burst with a deluge remembered years after.
"We'd better tell Santa this pair's still awake,"
laughed Mum, adding, "That was a rude noise to make "
We stayed in convulsions; as they left the room
Mum's girlish giggles came back through the gloom.
We finally slept, but when morning dawned bright
we leapt to our stockings and found them packed tight
with apples and oranges, and toys made from wood,
plus six pennies, brassoed, to make them look good

The presents were meagre, but we were impressed
knowing that Santa was doing his best.
A war was in progress and Dad home from sea
was quite the best present for Tommy and me.
When I think of that Christmas, the laughter comes yet
but closely behind it comes tears of regret.

I'm the only one left from that memorable night
we huddled in bed filled with wonder and fright.
till Dad's body-function came mellow and free
And left priceless memories for Tommy and me.

from
MEMORIES OF YORK STREET
(1991)

LYRICAL MEANDERINGS

I like to read the poems of Lord Byron,
and Masefield fills me with a sense of awe,
yet I'm equally at home with confrontations
that turn out to be physical and raw.
My temper has been tempered by the seasons
that come and go like images on glass,
but the coldness of my fury has caused problems,
for I never was a man to let things pass.

I love the vocal phrasings of Sinatra
as he sings lyrics written by the great.
Banality is banished by this genius—
give him the words and poems he'll create.
Like me the guy is partial to good likker,
and pleasured by the sight of a pretty lass.
When trouble tapped his shoulders, he just shrugged 'em,
'cause he never was a man to let things pass.

My spare time's spent creating or composing,
the pencil never seems to leave my hand.
Although my body's sitting here before you,
my mind's relaxing on some foreign strand.
I like to drink strong ale and Southern Comfort,
but you'll never find Scotch whisky in my glass
except when I'm remembering the bad days,
when I never was a man to let things pass.

I like to watch good boxers ply their talents,
using brains as well as brawn and fist.
I've lost the killing instinct bred in brawlers,
and let me tell you something, it ain't missed.
But in my cups I'm prone to being stubborn,
though I'm old, I'm still as bold as brass.
But now I let my pen do all the fighting,
'cause I never was a man to let things pass.

IT'S SAD WHEN GROWN MEN CRY, OR *WHAT GOES ON BEHIND THE CLOSED DOORS OF THE NORTH BELFAST CRUSADERS SUPPORTERS' CLUB*

Men gather for all reasons, to drink or shoot the breeze.
In other words, they like some time to do just as they please.
In the company of cronies, in a pleasant atmosphere,
far away from the better half, in a clubroom they hold dear.
Some guys get hooked on snooker, whilst others jog or run,
we support Crusaders, but lately it ain't been fun.
We bunched-up for an ouji board. Each week we gather roun'
and loudly chant in unison: *Don't let our team go down.*
Despite our dedication, we never seem to gain,
except for the odd occasion, our prayers have been in vain.

We sent for the Ayotollah who commenced to scream and shout.
It didn't help our forwards, but he wore our prayer-mat out.
We spoke to Derek Wade last week. He wasn't pleased at all
when we asked if Bobby Savage could build a wailing-wall.
We wear sackcloth and ashes, whilst praying for a win.
For years we've banged on Heaven's Door, but there's never
    no one in.
Johnny Wallace wrings his hands and is often heard to say,
"If we had a Tapper Davis, my hair wouldn't be so grey."
"Aye," replies wee Whitey, "Just think what we could do,
if we had a man between the posts as good as Dave Agnew."

We mope about the boardroom, every other Friday night.
We talk about the old days and fly on fancy's flight.
One night when very desperate, we phoned-up Brian Clough,
he listened quite politely, then told us to "**** off!"
"Oh, for a Leo McGuigan," sighs Tommy McAteer.
Although he came from Celtic, the Shore-men held him dear.
There was also Jimmy Simpson, a man of skill and flair,
way back in the fifties, when our treasurer had hair.

"I think," said Harry Davison, with a sly sarcastic dig,
"if we get relegated, we should buy yer man a wig."
That woke Bobby Savage, He surfaced with a yell,
"That's the best idea you've had. Can I have one as well?"
McAreavy, Boyle and Savage, Tynan, Patton, Stead.
Every week they reminisce and dream of days long dead.
There's a couple of foreign geezers, they talk in a funny way,

whilst knocking back Newcastle ale and Tudor crisps all day.
So it goes each meeting: we moan and dream and weep
and fantasise of a forward who could dribble, score and sweep.
We spoke to Dr. Paisley, he almost blew a fuse.
Saying "No way could I help you—shure I support the Blues."

So if we have our eyes closed as we eat our chip and chick,
don't think we're in the process of a quick and crafty kip.
As North Belfast Supporters, we're begging Him on high,
please keep us out of the bottom two, or we'll have to re-apply.
Lord, let a team of Angels descend on Seaview's groun',
gown them in the red and black and let them go to town.
Annihilate Glentoran ... Kick the Blues aroun',
Let this be their war-cry ... Don't let the Crues go down!
I'm gonna have to finish. You can see the reason why.
My tears have started flowin' ... Ain't it sad when grown men cry!

TALE OF A TENNER

There's an incident in my memory that's enshrined in a gentle mist.
I trot it out when the crack is good and I'm close to gettin' pissed.
It happened many years ago in the winter of fifty-five.
It concerns some guys who were pals of mine, and most of 'ems
    still alive.
We earned our corn in the Spencer dock where we handled spuds
    all day,
we checked and stacked till the sheds were packed, or the ship
    had sailed away.
There was Nicklo, Bennett, Whitey ... plus a guy who played football,
me and a chubby checker, whose name I can't recall.

The night was wet and dismal, as we trudged up Whitla Street.
The day'd been hard and hectic, and everyone was beat.
The carriers were knackered, the checkers' heads were turned.
Our throats were choked with spud-dust, in our bellies fires burned.
We headed for the Sportsmans' Arms to cadge some drink on tick.
There wasn't the price of a physic among that hard-up clique.
That's when a fella stopped us and shook Hump Bennett's hand.
"I'm glad you were my witness, for the lies you tole were gran'.

"My case came up this mornin', an' I got six hunnert quid.

Would you accept this tenner for doin' what you did?"
Bennett answered, "Thanks pal, you've really turned up trump."
He looked a lot like Bogie. That's why we called him Hump.
He took us over York Street to the Gibraltar Bar.
We couldn't wait to wrap our fists around a welcome jar.
Nicklo, Bennett, Whitey, and the guy who played football ...
Me and the chubby checker, whose name I can't recall.

We ordered double whiskeys chased by Red Heart stout.
The waiter's eyes turned glassy when we yelled the order out.
"Shure that wud cost a fortune," he cried with a puzzled frown.
"Wud ye decorate the mahogany before I bring it down?"
When Bennett flashed the tenner, his eyes lit with delight.
"Sor," said he, "I hope your party stays in here all night."
A tenner in that era was like a hundred now
and that was why the waiter commenced to scrape and bow.

Each pound had twenty shillings, each shilling twelve big pence.
Compared to what we have now, its power was immense.
A pint was one and sixpence, all spirits three and two.
Whitey ordered a double rum and a bowl of Irish stew.
I called a salad sandwich, and a beer to wash it down.
Nicklo's double sherry cost a mighty half-a-crown.
Big Albert ordered six boiled eggs and a pint of Double X,
He'd a match next day at the Oval and needed to relax.

Egg and onion sandwiches and whiskey by the ball
was ordered by the checker, whose name I can't recall.
The waiter totted up the bill as we drank the likker down,
saying, "One pound six an' tuppence is the damage for that roun'."
Bennett waved the tenner saying, "Get yerself a tot."
The waiter answered, "Thank you, sir, I'll have a whiskey hot."
The next round was all half-ins, chased by Red Heart stout.
It came to a pound and tuppence, which Bennett handed out.

The footballer was starving, and he began to gripe.
Hump went round to the butchers and brought back cheese
     and tripe.
I gradually got blutered, as the alcohol took hold.
Nicklo kept me upright, when my legs began to fold.
Big Albert left the table and lay down on the floor,
presumably to dream about the goals he hoped to score.
Whitey started homeward reciting Dan McGrew.
He staggered into Dock Street and threw up the Irish stew.

Scoffing raw black-puddings and whiskey by the ball
was the chubby little checker, whose name I can't recall.
Bennett left the premises to take his girlfriend out.
They supped hot Irish coffee scorning mundane things like stout.
He woke up wrecked next morning, and feeling quite bereft,
'til he opened up his wallet and found he'd four quid left.
It's hard these days to fathom exactly what we did ...
Six men drank and ate their fill and only spent five quid.

All were pissed or rightly and walked like livin' dead.
One poor soul was found asleep in the nearby Chapel shed.
I told that story lately in a large downtown hotel.
The punters sighed with envy, but the waiter broke the spell.
He walked across plush carpet and set our order down,
saying, "This is 1990 and the damage is ten poun',
A tenner has ten singles each worth one hundred pence,
there's no such thing as half-a-crowns so talk a bita sense.

"Forget yer Barney Dillons, yer sprazies an' cat's eyes.
Show the world a ten-bob note an' see how much it buys."
His tone was cold and scornful. "Stap livin' in the past.
Those days have gone forever," was his final icy blast.
Suitably admonished, I felt a trifle trite.
My company was silent—we all knew he was right.
Returning to the present I didn't find it strange
when he pocketed the tenner and said there was no change.

My mind returned to York Street and that day so long ago.
I saw the smiling faces of those pals I used to know,
Nicklo, Whitey, Bennett, and the guy who played football ...
plus me and the chubby checker whose name I can't recall.

DAVY AND ME
written to remember Uncle Davy, who, as they say, was some pup.

Davy and me! Now there was a team,
up to the moment he ran outa steam.
We were moochin' some pruck in a Pollock Dock shed,
when he crashed to the ground and in minutes was dead.
I don't want to dwell on the sordid details

of how death came quickly and all it entails,
I'd rather remember the good times we had
though he was a grown man whilst I was a lad.

Our friendship was formed in the flame of a fight
when he and I set on each other one night.
I've forgotten the insult that caused us to spar
but the battle half-wrecked the American Bar.
Next morning I surfaced, too fuddled to think.
The whole of my being was craving a drink
and just like a compass is drawn to a star,
I hauled myself down to the old Yankee Bar.

"Denis," I croaked to the Host, who was grinning,
"how did I do? Was I losing or winnin'?"
"I'm sorry," he chuckled, "but I missed the fight.
Why don't ye ask that oul fool on yer right."
I looked and saw Davy was propping the bar,
stale blood congealed on an ugly scar.
He burst into laughter at my swollen eye,
as Denis laughed, "Right now, who's goin' to buy?"

We drank from the bottles. It didn't feel right
but we'd smashed all his tumblers the previous night.
A close bond was formed by that first friendly drink
and never again was it pushed to the brink.
He loved centre stage and the people's attention.
The pranks he got up to are too much to mention.
He'd strut round the pubs like a real movie star,
preening and setting up drinks at the bar.

He dressed in great taste and was always in style.
As characters came, he was top of the pile.
He played all the angles and didn't hedge bets.
He went when his time came and had no regrets.
I think of him often and miss him a lot
whenever I sip at a pint or a tot,
'cause up to that day when he ran outa steam ...
Davy and I was a hellavua team!

THE BOSS OF THE TOWN

I was drinking with Jimmy McGregor, he once was the boss
of the town.
There wasn't a man who would face him, then he suddenly
quietened down.
The reason for that. He got married, to a sweet girl
called Jenny McGee.
I love her myself, but conceded. She wanted him, much more
than me.

The first time they met was in Barney's. Big Jimmy was wrecking
the place.
Then Jenny stormed in through the front door, a furious look
on her face.
It seems he had took on her brother and sent him home flat
on his back.
Wee Jen didn't stop for a statement, she stormed straight
into the attack!

Big Jim lost his feelings for combat, as Jenny's nails tore at his chest.
He guffawed and laughed at her efforts, and treated it all as a jest.
To cut it all short they were fated. And that put myself in a whirl,
for up to that violent meeting, Jenny McGee was my girl!

I went to Big Jim when I heard it. Though nervous, I put forth
my case.
Flinching each time he flexed muscle, expecting his fist in my face.
But I needn't have bothered to worry. Big Jim had turned gentle
and kind,
and nothing but sweet thoughts of Jenny, were floating around
in his mind.

Well anyway, I was their best man. The wedding was frantic and gay.
He looked like a king and her beauty was never as rare as that day.
But that was a couple of years back and Jimmy had changed
quite a bit.
His face bore the marks of a beating; the suit he had on didn't fit.

He sensed I was feeling quite puzzled and heaved a laborious sigh.
He said in a voice thick with passion; "I've just watched my sweet
Jenny die.
My Jenny was all I had longed for. I thanked the Lord each silvery
morn.

I thought I would be twice as happy, when our coming baby
    was born."

He then smashed my drink from the table and snarled, "If you'd
    had any drive,
you wouldn't have let me steal Jenny and Jenny would still be alive!"
My fist hit him, high on the cheekbone, he sprawled in a heap
    to the floor.
He rose to his feet and said tiredly, "C'mon laddie, try it once more."

My reason returned to me swiftly. Not one more attack would
    I launch.
Big Jim was the best in the city—against him I hadn't a chance.
But he didn't fight back. He just stood there, a beaten look bleak
    in his eye.
He gazed at the floor for a moment. I felt very sad for the guy.

"Laddie" His voice held a tremor. "My son and my Jenny are dead!
God couldn't take the big tough guy, so He took my loved ones
    instead.
But I'm gonna fool all in Heaven. Remember the guys I could chin?
Well, I'm gonna fight them all over, but this time I ain't gonna win.

"So take some more pokes at me laddie, I know I gave you a hard
    time."
His voice was too soft to be heeded for Jenny was still on his mind.
He turned on his heels and walked from me, and neither a word
    did we speak.
The moist in my eyes didn't stop me, from noting a tear
    on his cheek.

A week from the day that he left me, he died in a public house brawl,
drove on by the grief that possessed him, since he first heard sweet
    Jenny's call.
But I'll tell you for certain those bullies would not have put
    Big Jimmy down,
in the days before he met sweet Jenny, when he was the boss
    of the town.

UNCOLLECTED POEMS
(1957-1989)

ODE TO ALAN

The youngest in our family has got himself a job.
He's sittin' here like King Farouk, his feet up on the hob.
He's taken over my seat, the one for the man o' the house,
and I have got to sit here, as quiet as a mouse.

He's talkin' now in millions, he's the greatest guy alive.
He's gonna buy me ten fags each week instead of five.
He's walkin' round the kitchen, he's ready for the track.
You'd think to hear him talkin', he was never comin' back!

I think when he gets goin', he'll pay the nation's debt.
Maybe set me up in business—gosh, how lucky can you get!
But when TV comes commericial, and westerns reach the peak,
Will Cheyenne win the battle—against thirty-bob a week?

THE LUCK OF THE DEAL

In the Nugget, one cool of an evening (when the west was still
    golden and young)
round one of its whiskey stained tables, a dangerous atmosphere
    hung.
Two men looked across at each other, one scowled at the other's
    large grin.
The luck seemed to sit on his shoulders. His cards always raked
    the gold in.
Jack Beattie (his florid face flustered) was holding a wild tiger's tail.
The big man's fat face was a study, as he furitively bit at a nail.
His opponent gazed over the table as he rifled the cards in the deck.
His small narrowed eyes showed no feeling, as they probed
    at the perspiring Jack.
The waiters weren't doing much business, for men watched (with
    short-baited breath),
their boots shuffled soft throught the sawdust, as around the two
    players they pressed.
With dextrous fingers the cowboy tossed pasteboards across
    the soft deck.
The gold that had piled up beside him showed the player deserved
    some respect.

The light of a thousand bright candles shone down from a large
    chandelier,
as the cowpoke examined his own cards whilst pensively sipping
    a beer.
Jack glared at him, eyes brimmed with hatred, remembering that
    long hours ago,
he'd been drinking good Scotch in his office (and tossing a wide
    loop at Flo).
A croupier had rushed in to warn him of a guy who was running
    amok—
he'd dazzled the dealers with aces, and more than one bank
    had been broke.
When Jack learned the guy had ten thousand, and was steadily
    piling up more
he figured he'd fleece the dumb sucker (and then have him kicked
    out the door).
But alas! all goes not as you want it, and Jack found the cowboy
    no fool,
but a sharp-witted, shrewd-thinking gambler, who bet high and knew
    every rule.
The cowboy went out for a clean-up, his eye on Jack's fast fading pile.
He raises the bet feeling happy (not noticing Jack's fleeting smile).

Jack's bankroll is just about gone now, he deals out the cards
    that are due.
He takes one himself and nods grimly after giving his enemy two.
The cowpoke then shoves in ten thousand (and gives the fat man
    a quick leer).
"I'm bettin' the lot then I'm takin' the pot an' gettin' to hell
    outa here!"
Jack's forehead is perspiring freely, he knows he can't cover the call.
The saloon's about all he has left now (without that he's nothing
    at all).
Checking his cards for the third time, he sees that he holds
    a full house.
He'll bet the saloon, win his dough from the goon, and then put
    his fist through the louse.
He calls for a pencil and paper, and scrawls out a short IOU,
He throws down a house roofed with aces. Then asks with a grin
    "What have you?"
He finds that the man's eyes have left him. They rest on a guy
    to his right.
A tall guy who's bearded and dusty (and spoiling like hell for
    a fight).

The cowboy, his eyes flashing fear now, glared at the man dressed
    in black,
as the man rasped (his throat dry with trail dust), "For two years I've
    followed your track.
You're a saddle-tramp, spawned by the devil. You've murdered
    and cheated and lied,
so I'm playin' the part of the Lord now an' thinkin' it's time
    that you died."
The seated one snarled out a wild oath, "You always did talk
    a good fight."
Then swiftly he reached for his pistol. His opponent was faster
    than light.
Five rounds tore the life from his body, he slid with a scream
    to the floor.
The black-bearded man sheathed his weapon and backed slowly
    out of the door.
His calm exit broke the strained silence, Jack knelt by the bullet-torn
    man.
He called out "Free beer at the bar boys", then lifted the dead
    player's hand.
He stood all alone at the table, and watched as they made
    a mad rush.
He smiled as he looked at the death cards; a nine ten jack queen
    king straight flush.

He narrowed his eyes at the body, as he called for the funeral truck
(His morale overcome) he scowled at the dead bum, saying
"Some folk get all the good luck."

THE TIRED GUN

In the long drawn light of a summer night,
many years ago,
in an oil-lit bar, gently chewing a cigar,
sat an old grey wolf called Joe.
The snowy flush at his temples,
the hollowed eyes of a ghost,
the well-worn gun and the long lucky run,
said he was faster than most.
He sat there, nursing a whiskey.

A man feeling lonely and sad.
The tired eyes reflected a wry smile
as he thought of the tough life he'd had.
Five years with a badge down in Deadwood—
With that any man could be proud.
The wise guys who faced the thin gunhawk
all finished up wearing a shroud.

Remembering was all he had left now.
The killings had filled him with shame.
He wondered how long he would last now,
a slow moving man with a quickdrawing name.
His eyes left the dimly-lit doorway
and fell on a boy drinking rye.
He was drinking real fast
like each drink was his last.
He'd a dangerous gleam in his eye.

His voice held a shrill note of boyhood,
when he roared, "I'm called Jamie Greer.
I'm a pretty good gun ... I won't run from no son,
and I'll face any man sitting here."
The old gunman watched as the waddie,
a tall glass of rye in his hand,
began to entreat of the good men he'd beat
spilling tough blood all over the land.

The gun-hung kid finished his drinking,
then looked round at Joe with a glare.
"They tell me you're hot, but I'm sayin' you're not,
so come on, step outside if you dare."
Joe grunted and gazed at the gunnie.
The deep grey eyes didn't show fear.
He said, "Son, I've come far just to smoke this cigar.
I don't want no showdown in here."

Greer eyed the men in the bar-room
and knew if he played his cards right
he could blast the old man with a flick of his hand
and be drinking on credit all night.

That boy saw only the cover,
he didn't delve down deep enough.

He just saw an old guy, a beat look in his eye,
and decided to call the man's bluff.

Fingers caressing his gunbutts,
he spoke with a confident rasp. "Listen you fool
if that gun you don't pull
then you'd better start breathin' your last."
The old man sat still for a moment,
then pulled the worn gun from its sheath.
He looked at the chipped walnut handle,
and spoke in a voice filled with grief.
"I've flashed this old gun from its holster
in Tombstone and Abilene town.
I've faced up to many a fast draw,
then helped plant him into the ground.
When the gunsmoke had cleared I was standin'
an' wonderin' why it should be.
But I fought to preserve law an' order,
an' maybe the Lord stood with me.

"So I'm thinkin' it over real careful.
I'm thinkin' it over real well.
If it comes to the bit I don't think I could sit
on this seat whilst you blow me to hell."
The cowpoke, face flushed with excitement,
backed off, standing square, feet apart,
snarled, "Get offa that chair. C'mon get outta there,
an' say when you're ready to start."

The old one, his face lined with sorrow,
said in a voice filled with care,
"When you fall on your face
an' find hell's a warm place,
just remember you sent yourself there."
The watchers moved back, out of gun range.
The grey one stood calm and serene.
The young man was flexing his fingers.
They seemed like two men in a dream.

The young man said, "Pop, you can call it.
I'm waitin' an' ready to draw".
A silence had fell and the watchers could tell
the tension was making nerves raw.

Both men stood eyeing each other,
then Joe sent his hand flashing down.
Before the young guy could clear leather,
he was thrashing about on the ground.
He knew he was beat from the first shot.
His gunhand came up much too late.
He lay on the floor cursing wounds that were sore,
with nothing to do now but wait.
The wait didn't take but a minute,
from three holes in his chest his life drained,
and soon just a bullet-torn body
was all of the youth that remained.

The victor reholstered his pistol,
and ordered a tall glass of rye.
He sat in a trance at the table,
then once more he uttered a sigh.
"I've had just enough of this killin',"
he said in a voice tired and sad,
"but what can be done when boys carry a gun
an' drink likker that drives a man mad?
So now one more notch on my gunbutt,
it sure fills a guys heart with grief ...
But mebbe next town, I'll be the one down—
only then will I get some relief.

SONG OF MYSELF

A fool who wanders lonely through an empty barren street.
A man who hasn't friend or love, or a thing to make life sweet.
Alone and empty-hearted, in an orchard of regret.
A fool who with an axe of words cut each blossom that he met.

Time was when this fool's garden abounded with garlands of friends.
But, mark you, the stoutest of flowers untended,
will soon find how quickly life ends.
I left my flowers unguarded, I thought that I just didn't care.
But now that I long for my blossoms ...
My garden of friendship is bare.

MIDNIGHT

I love to walk at midnight, when the traffic's more subdued.
The glare of a lonely street lamp can make a man feel good,
feel glad to lose the memory of the daylight's frantic throng,
and wander in the warm glow of a night that's fresh and long.

A cigarette tastes sweeter when you smoke it in the dark.
The sleeping trees all whisper as you wander in the park.
A far-off clock chimes faintly on some steeple tall and grey.
Belisha beacons blink and light the lonely traveller's way.

A watchman's fire, its coal aflame, burns with a soft red glow.
He'll talk awhile with a cheery smile and watch solemnly as you go.
An unassuming soft breeze sweeps the cobwebs from your brain.
The world is asleep and silent except for the wail of a train.

The gently falling raindrops wash the sorrow from your eyes.
A flock of seabirds swiftly float across the troubled skies.
The moon speeds through the white clouds like a frightened
    golden fawn
and soon the red-rimmed hills will mark the coming of the dawn.

PICTURE MY FACE IN THE CROWD

When the guests assemble and the banns are read,
when you stand with your pretty head bowed,
when the organist deftly caresses the keys,
try to picture my face in the crowd.

When the minister quotes from his Bible,
as your lover stands tall, flushed and proud,
when he slips the gold band on your finger,
try to picture my face in the crowd.

They tell me that faith can move mountains
and though you've forgot all you vowed,
when you walk down the aisle,
at a vacant pew smile,
and picture my face in the crowd.

WHO

Who stood by me in sickness and trouble and health?
Who's sure to get a goodly sum, should I come into wealth?
Who always says "Cheer-up pal" when the cards don't fall my way?
Who always gives me courage to live another day?
Who loves me like a brother? Who cries when I am sad?
Who says he'll try to get me the things I never had?
Who'll let no man walk on me, who'll fight for what I own?
Who will I thank for helping me when I am older grown?
Who smiles and says tomorrow will bring a better sun?
Who'll laugh in all their faces when the long, long fight is won?
Who cheers me up when things look black?
Who wipes my tears, who pats my back?
Who says rise, each time I fall?
Who deserves the best of all?
Who'll be master in the end? ...
Who'll remain my greatest friend? ...
Myself!

MY BOYS

I'm gonna cram my kids with learnin',
I'm gonna fill their heads with facts.
They ain't gonna be a bum like me
humping those potato sacks.
I'm gonna teach 'em the worth of money.
They'll save every shillin' an' pound.
They ain't gonna play the horses,
they ain't gonna throw it around.
'Cause my dad had ideals when I was fifteen,
I told him to go to Hell.
I wanted work that was fittin' for a man.
I found it slingin' oyster shell.
But I'll whip those boys if they go for the joys
of whiskey, women an' fights.
I'll thrash 'em red till the knowledge in each head
eventually kindles an' lights.
They'll never know the doubtful thrill
of a shirt soaked grey with sweat.

They'll never sling timber in a snow storm,
they'll never go home cold an' wet.
They'll live from the sweat of other men.
I'll bully an' threaten an' rave ...
Only when they sit on top of the world,
will I lie still in my grave.

WILD WILD JAKE

He gazed at the door marked County Sheriff, opened it and strode
    in.
The sheriff growled from behind his desk, the young man forced
    a grin,
saying, "Pardon me, my name is Wright. I work for the Washington
    Wire.
Is it really true that you outdrew and captured Jake Maguire?"
Looking somewhat puzzled, the sheriff replied with a grin,
"Nobody outdraws that owlhoot, a company of troops brought
    him in."
Wright's smile hung on rather weakly, he frightfully peered
    at the cell.
The lone inmate glared at him fiercely. The young fellow didn't
    feel well.

Summoning up all his courage, he walked stiffly towards the cell
and said in a voice thin and nervous, "Would you have a story
    to sell?"
Jake Maguire seemed slightly startled, then nodded and scowled
    at the 'stray'.
"To tell you the truth that depends, son, on how much you're willing
    to pay."
They reached a price after much bickering, and Jake started off
    with his tale.
The young man sat spell-bound and silent, as Jake once again rode
    the trail.
"Do you know by the time I was twenty, I'd notched-up my gun
    twenty times.
I was wanted in Maine and Missouri. Abe Lincoln was told
    of my crimes.

"I fought for the North in the big war, although Abe would call me
    a fake.
They say Lee told Lincoln years later, 'You'd never have won
    without Jake.'
A tall guy called Earp ruled in Tombstone, a ganglin' quick-drawin'
    gent,
and nobody threw any wide loops unless it was with his consent.
Well, being a sort of a drifter, I landed in Earp's stompin' ground.
Before I'd unsaddled my pony, the word of my comin' got round.
I'd just downed a beer in Big Katy's, when Wyatt came hustlin' in.
He whispered to Kate, 'Get the Doc down, my chances with this guy
    are slim.'

The Doc entered some moments later, a'wheezin' an' coughin'
    like hell.
I said, 'Maybe you'd better vamoose doc, if you prod me you'll never
    get well.'
Wyatt stepped up and said coldly, 'We don't want no gunplay
    in town'.
I grinned in his face and said mildly, 'If that's so, you'd better
    back down'.
Just then a wild jasper named Hickok came amblin' through
    the back door
growlin', 'Some ranny givin' you trouble', then he saw me and said
    nothing more.
Earp spoke up, easing the tension, 'What say we all make a play ...
Maybe our three guns could take him and finish this legend today.'

I answered, 'Pretty good speech, Earp. I hope you're as good
    with your gun.
'Cos the Doc and Wild Bill don't look happy. In fact, they look ready
    to run.'
Earp swallowed hard and grinned weakly. Doc pleaded, 'Boys, let
    it stand,
as long as Maguire wears a gunbelt, he'll always be dealt a pat hand.'
Hickok was killed some weeks later, and Doc took a trip to the east.
I rode along to the Nations', my quick-roarin' colt never ceased.
The moment I hit the Big Muddy, I tangled with Chief Sitting Bull.
After I wiped out his whole tribe he christened me 'Jake Heap
    No Fool'.

A buck-toothed young gun-hawk named Bonney had a quick-drawin'
    man-killin' name.

So I sashayed right into the badlands, they all knew of Jake Maguire's
fame.
Billy the Kid as they called him instantly went for his draw.
I cleared leather minutes before him and cracked my big colt
on his jaw.
Then I came to this damn piece of prairie, the governer sent out
his troops,
They caught me in Blackwater canyon, attacking in hard-hittin'
groups.
The sheriff has give his opinion, but you'd better give mine
a fair crack:
two companies set out to take me, but only the one made it back."

The rattle of keys broke the silence. The sheriff cried, "Out you
come lad.
The militia's surrounded the courthouse, when Jake's hung,
we'll all sure be glad."
The boy left, his eager eyes shining, and ran to the telegraph post.
The sheriff looked in at the prisoner, and said: "You're a lyin' old
ghost.
You've never bin out of the Hoosegow, you never saw Billy the Kid.
You'd run for your life from an injun, yer a drunken old bum
on the skid."
He burst into loud raucous laughter, his eyes were a twinkling grey.
"I'd love to see that fellow's face Joe, when he hears we hung Jake
yesterday."
Getting his cut from the money, he pushed the wad into his belt,
roaring, "You must have been at the front, Joe, when the high cards
for liars were dealt."

WITH APOLOGIES TO PERCY FRENCH

Oh Mary this Belfast's one helluva place,
the likkering laws are an awful disgrace.
For into hell I would rather be cast
than to spend a dry Sunday in the town of Belfast.
The church has got such a tight grip on the folk,
shure they might as well be in the conquerer's yoke.
They've locked-up the pictures and closed up the pubs,
shure the only place left is the parks or the clubs.

In their tight little collars, they nose all around,
The church is the last place in which they'll be found.
But now they are trying to close up the clubs
And they're bound to succeed as they did with the pubs,
And if they succeed sure as eight follows seven,
They'll soon change its name to the city of Heaven.

FACELESS MAGEE

We sat one day, my cat and me.
My cat, by the way, is called Faceless Magee.
Whilst slightly imbibed and feeling quite free,
we started in talking, oul Faceless and me.
Don't get me wrong. As you will see,
the talking all was done by me.

Bathtubs, boats, peas and pods ...
I pause and smile as Faceless nods.
I said when cats roamed far Cathay
they hunted vermin every day.
Magee's black face lights as I talk.
He humps his back and starts to stalk.

I'm sure he'd keep the rats at bay
if he was out in far Cathay.
Magee and me had quite a chat,
he's pretty smart to be a cat.
His eyes shone wisdom, plain to see
he knows his onions, does Magee.

I told him 'bout the dog next door.
He spat and pranced about the floor
and flexed his paws as if to say,
"I'd fight that canine any day."
He rolled a little to the fire
and seemed quite ready to retire,

And so ended the tête a tee
that occurred last week
between Faceless and me.

THE BELFAST PUBLIC LIBRARY

Ghost to ghost! It was a wondrous day, the day I joined the library.
The bards of the world were in full array in the Belfast Public
    Li-bra-eh!
I wandered round this hallowed hall, lined with tomes on every wall.
No finer sight could I recall, in the Belfast Public Li-bra-eh .

Shelley's side by side with Yeats; Shaw, O'Casey, all the greats,
Shakespeare, Whitman, Byron waits in the Belfast Public Li-bra-eh!
For a mere half-crown I can rent out three of these books that mean
    so much to me.
Joyce, O'Neill and Thack-er-ee, in the Belfast Public Li-bra-eh.

I drink their words like a cat laps milk. The poems and prose are like
    honeyed silk.
I stood engrossed till the break of day in the Belfast Public Li-bra-eh.
With this wealth of verse in front of me, I murmer just one
    heart-felt plea:
Let me stay 'til I'm 93 in the Belfast Public Li-bra-eh.

A CONFESSION

I'd love to write a poem
of love and spring and youth,
    and paint a poignant etching
of a bitter moment of truth.
    Of butterflies and limpid eyes
and beauty to enchant.
    I'd love to write some flowery verse ...
But dammit all ... I can't.

I'd love to write a soliloquy
of judgement self-entrenched.
    Some deep divided principle
from which the truth is drenched.
    Of bridal gowns, cathedral towns
and life that feels no want.
    I'd like to wax real lyrical ...
But dammit all ... I can't.

WHEN THE BULLETS START TO FLY

I've heard the gaunches gaunching.
I've read the writer's word.
I've seen the snarling faces, fanatic and absurd.
I've watched the hatred mounting as statesmen glibly lie.
But they'll blandly state their innocence
when the bullets start to fly.

I've studied rabble-rousers as they wield their ugly art,
injecting killing notions in a patriotic heart.
I've mused at students squatting like piglets in a sty.
They'll soon return to studies
when the bullets start to fly.

I sigh as slick-tongued speakers weave
a curtain thick with hate
to blind with words the working-class,
who listen while they state
that civil disobedience must be the people's cry
Yet he'll deny all knowledge,
when the bullets start to fly.

I'm saddened watching children
attending separate schools.
Infants segregated by antiquated fools
who poison children's thinking
and won't let past days die.
Those bigots won't plead guilty
when the bullets start to fly.

I'm saddened by the malice
that's in my fellow man,
indignant at the actions of
those who hold command.
Incensed by politicians
whom God and law defy.
But I know who'll do the dying
when the bullets start to fly.

FEATURES SO FAMILIAR

In dreams I walked a foggy road, I carried neither pack nor load.
Across my path a stranger strode. His manner seemed familiar.
A swirling mist obscured the place, I felt my frightened pulses race.
I searched the grey mist for his face. A face that seemed familiar.

He snarled, "The fancy talkin's done, now we're alone
    an' one to one,
no more will you my friendship shun." His voice seemed
    quite familiar.
I sensed an inward kind of fear, and wished the night had been
    more clear.
Violence and hate lurked here, emotions so familiar.

Suddenly he lunged at me. The mist had cleared and I could see
his features as they blasphemed me. Dear God, they were familiar.
We fought until the break of day, hard and vicious all the way.
He left me bleeding and he walked away. With features so familiar.

AN ARAB OR A JEW

I'm sick of being Irish, sick of all it means
when reason has to perish as hate and terror
leans across a saddened province that's been blasted black and blue
By God I think I'd rather be an Arab or a Jew.

For this land of gifted scholars has taken to the gun
and this land of saints and poets has cast blood to the sun,
and the honesty of Ulster has capitulated too.
By God I think I'd rather be an Arab or a Jew.

But you can't commune with rabble
who are sick with fear and dread.
Or the sad and wet-eyed women who have
prayed and prayed and prayed
for an ending to this bloodbath that has cut our land in two ...
By God I think I'd rather be an Arab or a Jew.

THE SPECTRE

There's a spectre hangs around me, and whenever I lose hope
the shade will say in a ghostly way, "You can end it with a rope."
When the world gets on my shoulders and sags me at the knees,
I can hear him say in a friendly way, "You can plan your own demise."
But I've got strength of character, I'm damned if I'll go down.
I wouldn't take my own life, not if I owed the town ...
But then it's not all money. It's what beats in your heart,
and sometimes when I'm sad and low, I feel dejection start.

And likker doesn't help it none. In fact, it spurs it on.
You dream of what you once were and how your life's gone wrong.
Whilst the spectre hanging round you will talk just like a friend,
and say the world's a rat-race that only you can end.
He'll tell you death is cosy, like a heady pleasant drink,
and when dejection hits me, that's the way I feel and think.
And the spectre never leaves me, as I rise and struggle on.
Till I take my life or lose it ... I will sense his mournful song.

IN THE PATRIOTIC GAME

It's a time to load your weapon with a well-filled magazine
and lurk within the shadows, silent, dark, unseen;
to fill a man with bullets or set his home aflame,
in the all-consuming ardour of the patriotic game.

It's a time of being wakened in the middle of the night
by hard-faced men with rifles who strip you of your fight,
who beat you 'round the kidneys, at least that's what you claim,
in the all-consuming ardour of the patriotic game.

It's a barbed-wire ride to nowhere, with men stepping in your shoes.
A long ebb-tide that flows where there are no birds or booze.
But there's lesser men to bully and frighten with your fame
in the all-consuming ardour of the patriotic game.

It's a time of breathing fresh air and getting free at last.
Reporting to your O/C, before a week has passed.
Once more you load your weapon and go out to kill or maim
In a car filled with explosives, in the patriotic game.

It's a lightning flash to soft sand and a deeply buried box
containing half-a-carcass and fifty pounds of rocks.
Defective detonators on a job you thought was tame
have made another martyr in the patriotic game.

BROWN IN THE EDDIE CANTOR

"Brown in the Eddie Cantor,"
Eddie always said.
Every time I hear it,
I remember Eddie's dead!
He tried to teach me snooker,
in the Oxford, years ago.
I couldn't get the hang of it
and the games were long and slow.
He never lost his patience
and always said the same:
"Brown in the Eddie Cantor"
when we racked up a new game.
Eddie died in a bomb blast
when a York Road bar was hit.
Whenever I play snooker,
I swear I see him yet
setting up a new frame
when the last ball has been played—
"Brown in the Eddie Cantor."
That's what Eddie always said.

TOMMY ALLEN
Hairdresser to Gentlemen and their Sons

I was born in York Street, in a house no longer there.
When I was barely six months old, Tommy Allen cut my hair.
My dad took me to Dock Street and stood me on a chair.
I bellowed like a baby, when Tommy Allen cut my hair.

I went to school in Pilot Street. I didn't like it there.
I learned more in the barbers, when Tommy Allen cut my hair.

The old hands chatted freely about each world affair.
I got my education, when Tommy Allen cut my hair.

I went to fight the Germans in foxholes everywhere.
When I returned to Belfast, Tommy Allen cut my hair.
I sired some sons and daughters, the boys would girn and glare,
just the same as I did, when Tommy Allen cut their hair.

When grandsons came years later and stood upon that chair.
A nice old man with sideburns, Tommy Allen cut their hair.
My bones grew old and tired, my locks grew white and spare.
When I doddered into Dock Street, old Tommy cut my hair.

I'm ready for my Maker, old Tom's already there.
When I walk through those Pearly Gates,
I know who'll cut my hair.
I can see him in my mind's eye
as he toils away up there.
He'll clip my Angel feathers
and then he'll cut my hair.

DAVY

In sartorial splendour, he strides down the street
his long years belied by his twinkling feet.
Dressed to kill, dripping elegance par,
sauntering down to McIldowney's Bar.

From the peak of his eight-piece, pulled down low,
to the hand-made shoes with the spit-polish toe,
elegant trappings, without a doubt,
that show Big Davy is breakin' out.

His thickly waving hair is white, his eyebrows black
his brown eyes bright. His nose is fine,
unbent, unbroke. His grey moustache is a pencil stroke.
A mischievous grin sets his face alight.
He knows he's gonna get drunk tonight.

The belt adorning his ample waist
spells out his name, in the best of taste.

Initialled links show beneath his sleeve,
the price of his socks, you just wouldn't believe.

Sometimes he wears a colourful bow,
but today it's a beautiful scarf on show.
Silk, no less, with a polka-dot, and tied,
need you ask, in a carter's knot.
His safari-jacket is an oyster grey,
his trousers are toned to match, as they say.
A commanding figure, like a duke or an earl,
with his tan-coloured shirt, showing buttons of pearl.
A matching handkerchief flowers like a rocket
from his handstitched upper jacket pocket.
A large gold watch adorns his fob,
but he's not a man I would try to rob
for expensive rings which his fingers grace
would make a mess of any robber's face.
Seventy years and still quite spry
he'd murder any who dared to try.
Shoulders squared, arms swinging free,
this septuagenarian is a sight to see.

When he enters the bar, it erupts in a cheer
for Davy has broke out and gone on the beer.
Talking and drinking he wears us all out.
There's very few men like Big Davy about.
He drinks for a week till we're worn out and sagging,
then he changes his clothes and gets back on the wagon.

NED
for Barbara

He took the shilling at an early age and saw the world on
    a squaddie's wage,
reared three kids and a couple of lads—erred sometimes
    like many dads.
Hard work gave him a sturdy frame and he toiled long
    after retirement came.
He did the bets and got the pools, knew all the perms
    and all the rules,

but now his hands and his heart's at rest, he's gone where
    they only take the best.

He could dig out drains or build an extension. Do any job
    you'd care to mention.
Quietly using his hard-earned skill, he was seldom left
    with time to kill.
He also baked and could turn his han', to a teady farl
    or an apple flan.
At elbow wrestling he seldom lost, as young men found out
    to their cost,
but now his hands and his heart's at rest, he's gone where
    they only take the best.

Saturdays saw him in the Sunflower Bar, to be brought home
    stoned in a taxi-car,
but Sunday found the loveable sinner, carefully cooking
    the Sunday dinner.
He left us quickly, without goodbye, but in our hearts
    he will never die.
For we know he's described on the golden list as a treasured
    parent sadly missed
with big strong hands and heart at rest. He's gone where
    they only take the best.

THE STREETFIGHTER

Drink is brewed for gulpin', faces formed for pulpin',
foes beat 'til they fall or crawl away.
You've got a reputation for causin' depredation,
you've broke some bones and bodies in your day.

You're unsurpassed at fightin', your reflexes are lightning,
you rule the roost, with that they all agree.
Your head-butt's a sensation, your kick a revelation,
and you can find a crotch with any knee.

You tap the mug beside you, for although he can't abide you,
he'll part, in case you rearrange his teeth.
Though you're mostly on the level, when you
start to booze and revel, they're frightened of the devil underneath.

It's great to be the best one, alert for any test-run,
and watch 'im quiver as you stare 'im down.
That's why the drink is pilin'; they love to see you smilin'
'Cause things get kinda dangerous when you frown.

Drink is brewed for gulpin', faces formed for pulpin'.
You swagger, 'cause you're still the best around.
But you can't go on forever, and some young lad,
strong and clever, is waiting in the wings to steal your crown.

THE PEN IS MIGHTIER ...

The pen is mightier than the sword, the erstwhile scholar cries.
I told this to a bully once; he blackened both my eyes.
I tried to reason out the saw with this unruly breed.
He knocked me to the ground again. It seemed he couldn't read.
He'd never been to college. He'd never browsed through books.
He seemed to earn his living rearranging people's looks.
So if you meet with this type, for a diff'rent knowledge thirst ...
Brush up on your head-butt, and make sure you get in first.

NEWCASTLE BROWN

When little things irk me and life gets me down
I order a bottle of Newcastle Brown.
I find me a barstool and fill up my glass
with ale that's undoubtably top of its class.

The golden brown head looks deliciously cool.
The fellow beside me is starting to drool.
I sip the rich liquid and sigh with content ...
The money that bought it was money well spent.

I'm not claiming drinking will chase away care
for trouble is something we all have to share,
so whether you're pauper or king with a crown,
relax with the goodness that's Newcastle Brown.

SAYINGS

"We've got to keep all these Taigs in their place,"
says the well-to-do man with the steak-dinner face.

"We've got to blatter the Prods till they tire,"
says the untidy student, his eyes blazing fire.

"We mustn't cease sowing hatred and pain,"
says the thug in the hood as he murders again.

"We must ensure there is no place to run,"
says the police chief inspecting a new riot gun.

"We cannot win this insidious race,"
says the upper-crust major, afraid of disgrace.

"We must inform you that murder is sin,"
say the clerics whose churches are empty within.

"We must stay British whatever the price,"
says the widow whose husband lies colder than ice.

"The fight will go on," says the unashamed wife,
whose man has been jailed for the rest of his life.

"I'll grow up fast and I'll take my dad's place,"
says the young lad with tears on his grief-stricken face.

"I'll take the colours and carry them high,"
says the wee girl, heartbroken, but too proud to cry.

Ulster's a problem that stems from the gut,"
says the British MP with his eyes tightly shut.

He adds with a sigh: "It's frustratingly odd—
each faction thinks they are favoured by God."

NED KEENAN

Whenever I lift an orange,
Ned Keenan comes to mind.
He could judge their sweetness,
just by stripping off the rind.
"A sour one won't peel easy,"
he told me with a smile.
in the days he bossed the Orange boats,
and we helped him stack the pile.
An explosion in McGurk's Bar
left him and others dead.
Whenever I peel an orange ...
I always think of Ned.

THE VISIT
*written to honour the memory of late brethren of the Royal Ulster RAOB Lodge
No. 7868 GLNI, who will never return.*

I was sitting alone with my memories, and decided to go for a drink.
I boarded a bus for the city. It broke down, beside the Westlink.
I started to walk along York Street, wishing I'd brought my own car,
when I noticed a dimly-lit building that stood with its front door ajar.

I stopped for a moment and pondered—the place looked familiar
    to me.
Yet all of the buildings in York Street had been knocked down in '73.
The darkened door beckoned me to it. I felt neither panic or fear.
A sudden sensation of friendship hovered uncommonly near.

I pushed the big door till it opened and had a quick furtive look.
I was drawn up the shadowy stairway, like a fish on the end of a hook.
Even before I came to it, I sensed there would be one more door.
I knocked it the way I'd been taught to, in the sweet golden days
    gone before.

A slot opened up in the middle. I saw a familiar face smile.
I muttered some words to the brother whom I hadn't seen
    in a while.
The door opened up as he beckoned, a light seemed to shine
    from above.
I felt a warm surge of emotion, completely surrounded by love.

Tommy O'Toole was the Tyler, he gave me a cheery hello.
Big D.A. sat in the corner, complaining about his big toe.
Stewart was taking the minutes, Albert was doing A.B.
Joss wrote my name in the Charge-Sheet.
Duncan Cairns made room for me.

Victor made sure I was signed in, everyone seemed very pleased.
Bamber, his'bowl' at the ready, gave me a handful of 'Dees'.
As I gazed at the faces around me I heard the lodge-door get
    a blatter,
then our Tommy entered the Lodgeroom and gave me a big pint
    of Gatter.

Oul Sam McMaster was Primo. He smiled as I drank the first toast.
John Harrison giggled with laughter, and Bob Brown stood in
    for Mine Host.
McCluskey was at the piano, fingering out a nice tune.
Our Tommy got up and rendered a tune that he loved called
    'Blue Moon'.

Wee Harry Cowan came over and gave me some elder and tripe.
Jim Millar reached me some pickles, and a big lump of cheese
    that was ripe.
Millar then sang 'Tattoed Lady', Stewarty sang 'Lucky Old Sun'.
Oul Charlie sang of 'The Coachman'. Everyone joined in the fun.

For what seemed like ages we frolicked, singing and drinking our fill.
Gatters came in by the gallon, Junipers flowed by the gill.
All of a sudden came closing. I took a last sip from my drink,
then stood with my brother and brethern
and helped them to form a true link.

They thanked me for paying the visit and asked me to pass on
    their love,
saying they'd be there to greet us when we knocked on the Big Door
    above.
They turned sort of misty, then faded, waving to me as they went.
As brother by brother filed past me, I wondered what all of it meant.

I felt someone shaking my shoulder and quickly awoke from my
    doze.
I glanced at the clock on the mantle. It told me the Buffs would
    be closed.

"I would have wakened you sooner," my wife said, her eyes all
  agleam,
"But I hadn't the heart to disturb you for you seemed to have had
  a nice dream."

I tried to adjust to the moment and felt a sad tremor of pain.
Those faces still floated before me, I knew I would see them again.
Now when we toast 'Absent Brethren', I think of that Lodge
  up above
which all of us one day will visit in the Spirit of Brotherly Love.

THE WITCH
for Joanne

One night I was reading a comic
whilst lying tucked-up in my bed.
A pale moon shone in through the window.
It lit up our gardening shed.
I glanced now and then at the window
and watched the stars twinkle on high,
when suddenly into my vision,
I saw something shadowy fly.

It landed on top of our shed-roof,
I pressed my face up to the pane
and watched as a witch on a broomstick
strove to get airborne again.
Dressed all in black from her cocked hat
to the toes of her long high-heeled boots,
she screamed at the motionless broomstick,
and pulled out her hair by the roots.

I ducked down beneath our back-window
till only my eyes could be seen.
Her face was all withered and wrinkled,
and bathed in a shimmering green.
She took from her pocket a parchment,
and chanted what seemed like a spell.
When the broomstick stood up to attention,
she uttered a triumphant yell.

She suddenly looked at my window;
I heard her voice cackle, then call:
"Can't stop to talk to you, dearie.
I'm late for the Hallowe'en Ball."

MY MOTHER

I carried my mother, as she carried me,
and placed her where she long had wanted to be ...
At one with my father and now they're both free.
I carried my mother, as she carried me.

I carried my mother and thought of her life—
a widow much longer than she was a wife,
with five frightened children who cried at her knee.
I carried my mother, as she carried me.

I carried my mother that dark winter's day
and buried her ashes beneath the cold clay.
I planted a rose for the whole world to see ...
When I left my mother, I left part of me.

THE TREES

God made the earth and the seas, then frowned
when He saw it was arid, barren all around.
Bland and colourless to a degree,
and so He decided to create a tree.
He pressed it into the grateful earth,
then kissed it gently, to give it birth.
He pinned on leaves of assorted green
and said, "That's the prettiest thing I've seen."
He placed some flowers around its roots,
and on its branches He hung fresh fruits.
A small bird hovered, then built a nest,
And that was the bit God liked the best.
He smiled at the sight then waved His Hand

saying, "Let there be trees all over the land."
And up they popped all over the place
as God put beauty on the earth's grey face.
He jaunted off to a nearby star
and viewed the work He had done from afar.
Because the sight gave Him so much pleasure,
He left the legacy for us to treasure.

THE WICKED LIKKER

When the wicked likker takes me and I'm feelin' kinda blue,
then my mem'ry starts a'flyin' and my thoughts run back to you.
When I think of how you left me, when I killed the love we knew,
then the wicked likker takes me and my thoughts run back to you.

Once you took my ring and told me you'd be proud to be my wife.
We found a little cottage where we planned to share our life
but I took the wicked likker and you couldn't stand the pain,
so you left me at the altar and our cottage in the lane.

Now the wicked likker takes me every time I hear your name.
I know my actions hurt you but I couldn't play the game.
I took the wicked likker and became too blind to see
I hurt you once too often and now you're hurtin' me.

So I take the wicked likker 'cause there's nothin' else to do.
I dream of when you loved me and I long to be with you.
But you've found yourself a new love and the best thing I can do
is to take the wicked likker until I've forgotten you.

THE BOUL SHORE ROAD BRAZILIANS
alias the 102nd Old Boys

Don't talk to us of legends that swirl in football's mist,
like Geordie Best and Pele, and others fame has kissed.
Don't dazzle us with anecdotes of skills that earned them millions—
They wudn't git a luk-in with The Boul Shore Road Brazilians.

We keep our tackles decent; we're hard and tough, but fair.
We're lethal on good surface, and magic in the air.
The power in our volleys, whenever we score goals,
often leaves opponents with a goal-net full of holes.

Dedication keeps us going; dedication, skill and strength.
Until the final whistle blows we'll run the pitches length.
We'll bend the knee to no one but if we're fairly beat
we'll offer hands of friendship 'cause we're noble in defeat.

Pride and the love of football is our fuel and our power.
Sometimes the heat of battle leaves us petulant and sour.
But when we reach the Somerton and share a well-earned drink,
we laugh away the rivalry that led us to the brink.

Don't talk to us of legends that swirl in football's mist.
Don't mention their devotion, especially when we're pissed.
Talent, fame and fortune gave them bank accounts of millions,
but not as much enjoyment as The Boul Shore Road Brazilians!

MEMORIES OF A WEDDING

On 5th August, 63, a taxi called for yer man and me.
For years he had frolicked, likkered and diced.
Now he was going to get himself spliced.
I wanted to stop for a drink or two,
but Harry said, "Brother, I must be true.
My love for Betty shines like a star,
but I must admit I could murder a jar."
So we stopped at the Bunch and lowered a few.
The bridegroom bought for the whole damn crew.
The crack was good 'til he sang a song.
That's when I reckoned we'd stayed too long.

As I wrestled him out, I heard a fella say,
"That was a terrible price to pay,
never before have I suffered such pain.
Get him out before he starts again."
As we sailed along Corporation Street
I have to tell you we looked a treat—

high-boy shirts and Chelsea boots,
slim-jim ties and cutaway suits.
Davison sat there, bronzed and fair,
he'd just that morning dyed his hair.
I muttered, "Let's stop for another drink."
He said, "As a best man, John, you stink!

"My one love's waiting at Sinclair's Church,
how can I leave her in the lurch?"
I made excuses to slake my thirst,
"Listen pal, you've got to be there first.
In the time between, we cud drink two barrels
so tell the driver to halt at Ma Carrolls."
How well I remember that unrehearsed stop.
Ma thought Harry was a plain-clothed cop.
The girls all thought he was Steve McQueen,
I saw a resemblance to Frankenstein.
But I wasn't working when the wedding came,
so I hadn't a throopenny piece to my name.

From a wad of fivers, he slipped me a few,
so I shouted, "He sings like Sinatra too."
I swear I'll never forget that day—
he stood on a table and sang 'All the Way'.
We left that pub in Great George's Street
with women swooning all over his feet.
One girl screamed as she followed us down:
"I'm yours Harry baby for half-a-crown."
He stood for a moment in the summer air,
then did his impression of Fred Astaire.
As he blew them kisses we sped to the church
where Betty was feeling left in the lurch.

To a screeching of tyres we disembarked
and sped to the altar where the bride was parked.
Betty and Hazel looked pretty and fair,
but I think him and me was the best lookin' pair.
What more can I say of that wonderful day.
He sang and he danced until they went away.
Some of the guests thought he went a bit far
when he took off his clothes on the roof of the car.
The honeymoon passed with comparative peace.
He went to Butlins and she went to Greece.

He swallowed the anchor for his Betty's sake
and got a good reference from Nelson and Drake.

It's twenty-five years from that day we danced there,
now the oul sea-dog is losing his hair.
"Harry," I tell him, "it ain't right to brood
just 'cause the Best Man is still lookin' good."
Just one more stanza and there I will end,
My brother-in-law has become my good friend.
I hope he'll forgive me for blowing the lid
off that wonderful day when he married our kid.

NOTES AND INDEX

Author's Notes

The Rose and the Blade (p. 19)
Written for the happy occasion when our son, Alan, married Mandy.
Naturally, I read it at the wedding.

Northern Ireland (p. 20)
A poem I am rather proud of. I put it together to the title tune of the
Rogers & Hammerstein musical, *Oklahoma*.

The Belfast Battler (p. 21)
Written to celebrate the deeds of an excellent boxer from Henry Street
in Sailorstown. It was followed by a prose article called 'Tommy Stewart:
The Story of an Uncrowned Champion'.

Listed Buildings (p. 24)
This poem was written to celebrate the pubs that were part of the York
Street legend. Some of us would gather and talk about them. As the years
rolled on we began to forget their names and owners. Near the end of
1991, I decided to put them all in verse for posterity.

Lament for an Arab (p. 28)
'Arab' was a derisory name applied to the casual dock labourers
although they had been on Belfast Dock since its inception. However,
like Mongomery's famous Desert Rats, they took it and made it a term
synonymous with hard work and tenacity. They could turn a boat
around faster than a typhoon at sea. The above poem is the story of their
demise.

There Are Men Like That (p. 33)
Celebrates the unassuming men who stood up to the bullies and tyrants
who would make us their slaves. This poem was read at a reading as a
tribute to shopstewards. Later, I saw it copied in a magazine changed to
unisex and titled 'There Are People Like That'. I wasn't pleased.

I Care for the People (p. 34)
The thoughts of a man for the working class to which I belong. It is
dedicated to the memory of Jackie Myers, a tireless crusader for workers'
rights, who came from Sailorstown.

The Old Man and the Sovereigns (p. 35)
A story told to me by Davy Whiteside.

It Didn't Hurt! (p. 39)
A true account of a fight I had gotten into with four hoods which
hospitalised me. My son, Mark, was there. Had it not been for him I
would probably have been kicked to death.

A Death in the Afternoon (p. 41)
Written after I took my dog, Prince, to the vet to be put down—an action I regret bitterly to this day. The poem was put together one night after I had drowned my sorrows in an effort to dull my conscience.

My Girl (p. 44)
Written for our thirtieth wedding anniversary, it was written to recall the day itself. A stormy relationship due to my stupidity, it has survived, not through any virtues of mine.

Sounds that Bring Me Pleasure (p. 43)
A possible song lyric, I think.

Jonathan (p. 46)
Written for my grandson.

Louise and I (p. 47)
Written for my granddaughter, Louise, to mark her third birthday.

Five Short Poems (p. 51)
These were written to introduce sections of my first collection, *Saturday Night in York Street*. Here I have put them together for ease of reference.

The Dark Bad Days (p. 52)
Written on the page of a checker's notebook in the Chapel Shed.

Casual Curses (p. 52)
As well as appearing in anthologies such as the *Ulster Reciter*, this poem was set to music by musician Maurice Leyden in 1988.

Jack (p. 53)
A blockbuster, the first draft was written in three hours. The first lines came to me on a Saturday morning as I drove home from work. My wife was waiting for me to take her out. I ran upstairs and said I wouldn't be long. I came down three hours later and the first draft was complete.

45 Earl Street (p. 61)
During the redevelopment of Belfast, many of the old streets were knocked down, destroying much of the community spirit in working-class areas. In this poem, I revisit the house I was reared in. It was knocked down in 1971.

Suckered (p. 63)
One of my most popular poems, it appeared in an anthology of pieces centred around drinking called *The Pure Drop*.

Little Helper (p. 65)
Dedicated to the small cargo hook which could be hidden in the palm

of one's hand. It is referred to in more detail in 'Lament for an Arab'.

Hell is the Houl of a Beg Boat (p. 69)
A poem written to remember the hard physical work attached to loading or unloading a ship's cargo.

The Tug-Boat Sailor (p. 70)
A humorous poem recalling six weeks I spent as a tug-boat hand on the *Southampton* which was the last of of the coal-burning tugs in Belfast. The Bannerman's was a cheap tawny wine.

My Daddy fought for Ireland (p. 78)
A poem reacting to the troubles.

A Jug of Barney's Wine (p. 79)
This poem was considered for recording by the Battlefield Band, but they didn't do it . It has proved to be one of my most popular poems.

York Street Flute (p. 81)
Written to remember the local lads of the area.

Belfast 69-76 (p. 82)
Used in the programme for Paddy Devlin's play, *Strike.*

Saturday Night in York Street (p. 83)
The title poem of my 1982 collection. The idea for this poem came to me as I sat aboard a sixty-tonne lift truck at the Knuckle. As I wrote I thought , "Wouldn't that be a lovely title for a book of poems."

The first two verses were used by the actor/producer/director Kenneth Branagh in the opening chapter of his autobiography, *Beginnings.* He also read the verses at the launching of this book in Belfast in 1990.

A Song for Barbara (p. 88)
The problems of being married to a guy in love with his typewriter!

Wage Negotiations York Street Style (p. 89)
This poem is based on a true story and explains itself. Life was hard then, in more ways than one, and sometimes one wasn't as tough as he thought he was.

I Am (p. 91)
A poem I am particurly proud of. It is a thoughtful little piece far removed from the hard work, hard drink, and hard times that permeate most of the other poems.

I'm Singing Just for You (p. 92)
Another attempt at a song lyric. Some day I may get around to trying to

hang a tune onto it. It reads well as it stands.

The Cure (p. 93)
Another attempt at humour, and perhaps a signal to show I wasn't taking myself too seriously. It is also true my own verse puts me to sleep. Not, of course, when I'm reading in public.

The Hardest Game (p. 94)
Written to honour a boxing legend from Belfast's Sailorstown called John McGreevy. This was one thing the mixed community agreed on. Jack Quinn—McGreevy's ring name—was possibly the finest boxing master to come out of the area. Denis Smyth asked me to pen this tribute when the old fighter died. I was very proud to be given the task and hope the short poem sums up how popular and talented he was.

A Wry Observation (p. 95)
Written to recall Uncle Davy's death with humour—which is how he would have liked it.

Cagney's Not Dead! (p. 96)
A tribute from a cinema buff to a legend of the silver screen.

The Actor (p. 96)
This poem was written when the first line came to me. I decided to follow it up and endeavoured to make it a piece of fun in rhyme. It rolls off the tongue, I hope. The story is, perhaps, secondary to this.

Christmas Street in York Street 1944 (p. 97)
A popular poem, this is based on a true event and fond memories.

It's Sad when Grown Men Cry, or What Goes on Behind the Closed Doors of the North Belfast Crusaders Supporters' Club (p. 102)
Our wish was granted. The club were not relegated that year and recently has gone on to win many honours.

The Boss of the Town (p. 107)
One of my most popular poems.

Ode to Alan (p. 111)
Written for my younger brother, Alan, who got his first job—as we all did in those days—at 14.

The Tired Gun (p. 113)
One of a series of western poems I have written. They were read recently on the Gerry Anderson radio show.

Song of Myself (p. 116)
I think I was somewhat depressed when I wrote this poem!

Midnight (p. 117)
This poem is a reminder of the lovely peaceful hours and days when a man could walk alone for miles without disturbance from anyone.

Picture My Face in the Crowd (p. 117)
An attempt at a song lyric, and a good one, I think.

My Boys (p. 118)
This was written some six and a half years before the first of my two sons, Mark, was born. They didn't heed me.

With Apologies to Percy French (p. 121)
Thirty years after this poem was written, everything is open on Sunday. All are filled—except the churches.

The Belfast Public Library (p. 123)
This poem was originally written for a character to recite in a short story which was later transformed into a play called *Pints and Politics*.

When the Bullets Start to Fly (p. 124)
This poem was published in the now defunct *Sunday News* in December 1968 just before anyone was officially killed in our current spate of troubles.

Brown in the Eddie Cantor (p. 127)
Dedicated to the memory of Eddie McMurray who was a pal of mine during my early days on the quay.

Tommy Allen (p. 127)
Written to remember the old family barber who cut our hair from the cradle to the grave.

The Streetfighter (p. 130)
Written to celebrate the lives of—and to mourn the passing of—the old type of Belfast streetfighter. Men who knew of honour and principle.

The Pen is Mightier ... (p. 131)
Another tongue-in-cheek effort, it came to me as I drove an opened-cabbed forklift truck through a blizzard in Belfast Harbour in what we would quaintly call 'the arsehole of nowhere'.

Newcastle Brown (p. 131)
Written to celebrate a good ale. I sent it to the company to see if they would use it for advertising. The director was impressed with it and sent it to their publicity people in London. I never heard another word.

Ned Keenan (p. 133)
Ned Keenan was a friend from my dock days when I worked at the potato

boats. An Irish Transport foreman docker, he was a kindly man and would sometimes give us a lie-on loading crates of oranges discharged in the shed we were working in. Just as we got to know quite a lot about the different brand potatoes we carried on our backs, Ned knew his oranges. He always comes to mind when I lift an orange, and I guess that's as good a testimony as any for a decent man.

The Visit (p. 133)
The Buffalo Order is a non-sectarian organisation which was sadly depleted by the bomb blitz on public houses in the early 1970s as most lodges used a consecrated room in the local pubs. It is still going strong though, but I'm sorry to say other commitments caused me to stop attending in the early 1990s. This poem was written with affection for fellow Buffalo brethren who have passed on, including my older brother Tommy and great pal Jim Millar.

The Witch (p. 135)
Written to amuse Joanne when she was a child. Now's she about to become a mother for the first time.

The Boul Shore Road Brazilians (p. 137)
Written at the request of my eldest son, Mark, who was playing football for the 102nd Old Boys. That year they won the cup. The club still recites the poem at annual 'do's.

Notes on dates

Over forty years much has changed and many of my poems stem from particular times and incidents. Therefore, in order to help place the poems more fully in their context, I list below the year of composition.

1959: *Ode to Alan* (p. 111); *The Luck of the Deal* (p. 111); *The Tired Gun* (p. 113); *Song of Myself* (p. 116); *Midnight* (p. 117).

1960: *Song of a Ship* (p. 73); *A Jug of Barney's Wine* (p. 79); *Picture My Face in the Crowd* (p. 117); *My Boys* (p. 118); *Who* (p. 118); *Wild Wild Jake* (p. 119).

1965: *Little Helper* (p. 65); *Skint Again* (p. 68); *With Apologies to Percy French* (p. 121).

1966: *Casual Conversation* (p. 61); *Suckered* (p. 63); *Fightin' Talk* (p. 64); *Faceless Magee* (p. 122).

1967: *York Street* (p. 66); *Sailorstown* (p. 68); *Tale of a Spud Boat* (p. 71); *Suckered Again* (p. 75); *The Man Inside* (p. 76).

1968: *Casual Curses* (p. 52); *The Dark Bad Days* (p. 52); *An Enlightened Frightened Fightin' Man* (p. 65); *Song of an Exile* (p. 91); *Boss of the Town* (p. 107); *A Confession* (p. 123); *Belfast Public Library* (p. 123); *When the Bullets Start to Fly* (p. 124).

1969: *Features So Familiar* (p. 125).

1970: *Jab and Move* (p. 77); *An Arab or a Jew* (p. 125); *The Spectre* (p. 126).

1971: *Jack* (p. 53); *45 Earl Street* (p. 61); *The Tug-boat Sailor* (p. 70); *What Does it Matter?* (p. 78); *My Daddy Fought for Ireland* (p. 78); *The Sportsman's Arms* (p. 79).

1975: *In the Patriotic Game* (p. 126); *Brown in the Eddie Cantor* (p. 127)

1976: *Belfast 69-76* (p. 82).

1979: *Hell is the Houl of a Beg-Boat* (p. 69); *Freedom Fighter* (p. 80); *York Street Flute* (p. 81); *Saturday Night in York Street* (p. 83); *Tommy Allen* (p. 127); *Davy* (p. 128).

1980: *Belfast Docks* (p. 73); *Ned* (p. 129)

1982: *Five Short Poems* (p. 51); *Sing a Song of York Street* (p. 84); *The Class of Sixty-nine* (p. 88); *The Streetfighter* (p. 130).

1984: *I'm Singin' Just for You* (p. 92); *The Actor* (p. 96); *The Pen is Mightier* ... (p. 131).

1985: *Wage Negotiations York Street Style* (p. 89); *I Am* (p. 91); *The Muse* (p. 92); *The Cure* (p. 93); *The Hardest Game* (p. 94); *Newcastle Brown* (p. 131); *Sayings* (p. 132).

1986: *An Oul Jobbin' Poet* (p. 87); *A Wry Observation* (p. 95); *Cagney's Not Dead!* (p. 96); *Ned Keenan* (p. 133); *The Visit* (p. 133); *The Witch* (p. 135); *My Mother* (p. 136).

1987: *A Song for Barbara* (p. 88); *Christmas in York Street 1944* (p. 97); *The Trees* (p. 136); *The Wicked Likker* (p. 137).

1988: *Davy and Me* (p. 105); *The Boul Shore Road Brazilians* (p. 137); *Memories of a Wedding* (p. 138).

1989: *I Care for the People* (p. 34); *The Old Man and the Sovereigns* (p. 35); *It Didn't Hurt* (p. 39); *I'm in Love with a Radio Deejay* (p. 42); *Sounds That Give Me Pleasure* (p. 43).

1990: *Lament for an Arab* (p. 28); *The Lecture* (p. 43); *Lyrical Meanderings* (p. 101); *It's Sad when Grown Men Cry, or What Goes on Behind the Closed Doors of the North Belfast Crusaders Supporters' Club* (p. 102); *Tale of a Tenner* (p. 103).

1991: *Listed Buildings* (p. 24).

1992: *The Rose and the Blade* (p. 19); *Song of a Son of the Old School* (p. 32); *Big Al* (p. 38); *The Rhyming Poet at Work* (p. 40); *My Girl* (p. 44).

1993: *Northern Ireland* (p. 20); *There are Men like That* (p. 33); *A Death in the Afternoon* (p. 41).

1994: *The Belfast Battler* (p. 21); *The Sailor* (p. 27).

1996: *Jonathan* (p. 46); *Louise and I* (p. 47).

1997: *Old Soldier* (p. 34).

Title & First Line Index
(first lines are in italics)